The Silence Between Us

Disclaimer

It is with relief, pride and trepidation that we share our story of the crises we lived through almost twenty years ago. It is our subjective version, and we respect that not everyone who was a part of that time will agree with what we experienced, saw or felt. But we can say that this is our precise recollection of the good, the bad and the ugly. We wrote it from diaries kept in the moment, as well as emails, letters and personal memories. This is our truth – not 'the' truth. And only part of our whole story. Many moments and events have been omitted, intentionally or not. We've changed names, obscured some details and occasionally used creative licence to respect privacy or shorten a long story. We hope not to offend or upset. Note there are some confronting descriptions and sad bits. Please seek support if you need to.

The Silence Between Us

a mother and daughter's
conversation through
suicide and into life

OCEANE CAMPBELL WITH CÉCILE BARRAL

Hardie Grant

BOOKS

Published in 2021 by Hardie Grant Books, an imprint of Hardie Grant Publishing

Hardie Grant Books (Melbourne)
Wurundjeri Country
Building 1, 658 Church Street
Richmond, Victoria 3121

Hardie Grant Books (London)
5th & 6th Floors
52–54 Southwark StreetLondon SE1 1UN

hardiegrantbooks.com

A catalogue record for this
book is available from the
National Library of Australia

The Silence Between Us
ISBN 978 1 74379 670 2

10 9 8 7 6 5 4 3 2 1

Cover design by Laura Thomas
Cover art by Angi Thomas
Typeset in 11/18 pt Sabon LT Std by Kirby Jones

Printed in Australia by Griffin Press, part of Ovato, an Accredited ISO
AS/NZS 14001 Environmental Management System printer.

The paper this book is printed on is certified against the Forest
Stewardship Council® Standards. Griffin Press holds FSC® chain
of custody certification SGSHK-COC-005088. FSC® promotes
environmentally responsible, socially beneficial and economically
viable management of the world's forests.

Hardie Grant acknowledges the Traditional Owners of the country on which we
work, the Wurundjeri people of the Kulin nation and the Gadigal people of the
Eora nation, and recognises their continuing connection to the land, waters and
culture. We pay our respects to their Elders past, present and emerging.

Oceane

To Cécile: for climbing many mountains with me, knowing when to say yes, making me resilient and courageous but also holding me in my vulnerabilities when it mattered.

To my little loves: with their snotty kisses, arms fiercely wrapped around me, and kicks in the ribs. Thank you for softening me, humbling me and motivating me to think bigger.

To Oma (1935–2019) and my whole 'blown in by the wind' family: for teaching me how to see something beautiful every day and for loving me completely.

And of course to you, my wife, Sarah: for your endless support and the monumental love you shine at me. Thanks for making it so easy to see something beautiful every day.

Cécile

To Silvana: for your quiet and steady presence.

To Odile: for being my best big sister.

To Maman: who did her best to manage big traumas with no help.

To Mamie: who taught me so much about life and coming through trauma.

And to all those who have walked a difficult path or had to watch a loved one walk such a path.

Foreword

This unique and important book is long overdue.

Oceane and Cécile's joint account of Oceane's suicide attempt as a teenager makes for a raw and gut-wrenching read. This is why people want to force the topic of suicide into the shadows, though it touches nearly all of us in some way. Oceane and her mother are courageous not only for their searing and poetic honesty but also for their willingness to challenge injustice and expose painful and humiliating experiences.

This beautifully written story reveals some of the underlying vulnerabilities, risk factors and triggers of suicidal behaviour, and the huge aftermath and secondary trauma for those directly affected: the person who survives and their closest family and friends. I personally know of many parents who are living with a suicidal young person and cannot get the help they need on a consistent basis. This book exposes us to their unremitting anguish, which is worse still if their child dies.

Suicide attempts are very common in young people. During this peak period of mental health risk, we have a limited capacity to withstand emotional pain, combined with major life and maturational stresses. Suicide is the greatest killer of young Australians, much higher than the road toll, yet society is only vaguely aware of this. The impact of COVID has only increased the magnitude of mental health issues and the importance of destigmatising and allowing conversations about suicide among families, friends and health professionals. The challenges of COVID – social isolation, anxiety and lack of control – are all themes that can be identified in Oceane's story.

The silence and ignorance surrounding suicide prevents effective action. Even some of the experts are afraid to tackle the issue head-on because of exaggerated fears of making the problem worse by opening it up to full public discussion.

But silence is never a good strategy. In this climate of taboo, far too many people are dying unnecessarily or being damaged through preventable suicide attempts. People are inhibited from confiding in others through shame, combined with a lack of avenues to access genuine help.

All health professionals who are in contact with distressed or suicidal people should read this book. The response to those presenting at emergency departments and mental health triage systems around the nation leaves a lot to be desired and in many instances causes further harm. We urgently need to invest much more heavily in reforms and expert specialised youth mental health care.

Only full and open discussion will lead to preventive programs that work and the right cultures of care on a scale proportional to this major public health issue.

While Oceane and Cécile have found healing through writing this testimony, they have also done something of huge importance in wider society by breaking the silence on suicide. They have done this without romanticising the issue; rather, they enlighten all of us.

Professor Patrick McGorry AO

Prologue: Thursday 17 August 2017

Cécile

My darling Oceane, I am gliding down the street on this sunny and crisp winter morning, on my way back to you after dropping your little Dominique at day care.

'Dominique has a new baby sister – Gabrielle!' I announced to his carer, my voice breaking with emotion.

Hard to believe it was only yesterday afternoon that I got your SMS: 'Labour has started. Come when you have finished work. No rush.' But of course I could not wait to see you. Your first pregnancy and birth! Two and a half years ago it was your wife, Sarah, who birthed Dominique, my first grandchild.

Only twelve hours since I parked my car in front of your home and let myself in through the front door. The family room was softly lit with candles, everything was tidy, the dining table had been pushed to the side to make room for the birthing pool and Gurrumul was playing in the background. You and Sarah had created an atmosphere of peace to welcome we had no idea who yet.

And there you were, in your thick navy-blue dressing

gown, totally focused on relaxing the best you could with each new contraction – Sarah right there with you, soothing and encouraging. You, my daughter, who fifteen years ago was so silent, who shut me out, who couldn't see the point in living, but is now surrounded by so much love and life, about to birth a baby at home, as I had birthed you. I had always wished but never dared to hope that this could be the life I would get to see you living.

My role last night was to get little Dominique to sleep and stay in the bed with him through your labour. I could not sleep, Oceane: my ears and eyes were with you as I heard Sarah and the midwives encouraging you, and you groaning, humming to yourself, showering, puking in the toilet.

Then around 5 am the noises suddenly changed. A wave of louder encouragement followed by a chorus of exclamations: 'The head is out!'

At that moment, Oceane, I could not stay away any longer. I came out of Dominique's room and there you were, sitting in the birth pool full of bloody water, your exhausted body reclining against its edge. You were holding a viscous little something on your chest. Oh the expressions on your face, Oceanette: cycling through pure bliss, laughter, tears, disbelief. 'I did it! I did it! Oh my baby!'

As I went to cradle your head with both my hands and give you a kiss of pure motherly love, my silent words were: *My daughter has given birth to her own tiny, perfect daughter. Life has won.*

15 years earlier

Cécile

Five days ago, my daughter failed to kill herself.

Fortunately, by some sort of miracle, her body or her mind or some mysterious force would not let her go. So my daughter did not die and in the end, I am a very lucky mother.

Only five days ago, she went on a twenty-four-hour rampage against her own life. She was very close to death when she called a friend and left the message:

'Bonnie, are you home?'

By chance, Bonnie got the message before it was too late, and told her dad who happened to be visiting. They drove her dad's car to the college's entrance, ran upstairs and found my daughter. They carried her down the stairs and drove straight to the nearest hospital.

They only just managed to save her, and so my daughter is being given a chance to find her will to live.

I found her three days later: because she was just over eighteen, the hospital had to respect her request not to notify her parents. A few days after that, she was scheduled and declared 'not sane of mind'. So, my not-sane-of-mind daughter could have died and I would not have been called to be with her in her last moments. A strange world of strange rules and protocols.

How did I find her, then?

I found my daughter because mothers sometimes know that something has gone terribly wrong. They just know it in their guts and cannot sleep till they have found their child.

It is 1 am and I, the lucky mother, am sitting up in bed. A mopoke is calling from the mountain. Sleep is not a proposition for me anymore. I have decided to use the quietness and spaciousness of the night to try to find some words. My daughter is standing on the edge of a cliff, still contemplating jumping off again, and I find myself in a state of total terror and powerlessness. Any movement or noise might push her over. On the other hand, not moving or saying anything might be her killer.

In this state, where thinking and feelings are frozen, language seems to have gone too: there are no more conversations in my head, with myself or with others. And if I have no words, how will I remember? And if I can't remember, this nightmare will probably stay frozen inside my head forever.

So I coax out the words and let them land on the paper.

Sunday 27 October 2002

Oceane

It is Sunday – nearly Monday really – and I have spent the last hours in a trance scrawling on an empty page in my diary. Writing in the tiniest letters possible so that it is illegible: 'I hate you I hate you I hate you I hate you I hate you'. Spiralling from the outer edge of the page, around the edge and slowly circling towards the centre.

This weekend is a jumble in my head and I keep leaping from one memory to another. Hearing Seth call out to me a few hours ago as I fumbled with the keys to get back into the building. The sheer panic overwhelming me at the sound of his voice, the sick tremor in my hands and stomach.

The afternoon launch for my grandma's book – her memoir describing being hidden and raped in a cellar in Paris as a child during the Holocaust. All that talk of sexual violence. I left feeling sickened. There was too much pain from my own experience of not feeling safe, from having my own boundaries constantly disrespected. The shame of thinking that what I had experienced was nothing like the years of rape and trauma she suffered, and yet having no voice for the discomfort caused by years of pats on my bottom, comments on my breasts. Being made to feel like my body was on display for the eyes and remarks of others. Like my body wasn't mine. How could I ever have spoken up about any of my shameful memories, knowing what she had endured?

And then there is the nauseous memory of Friday night. The college's annual dinner. I was barely present that night – so wrapped up in the darkness of my mind. There were speeches, and awards. Even though the master mispronounced my name ('Ocean') when I was nominated for college citizen of the year, I still felt something of a happy warmth creeping in, a feeling that maybe I am not as invisible as I think. And then the next nominee: Seth. What sort of cruel joke is that? How could they let him be nominated, especially alongside me? Why did they have the decency to say his name correctly?

I can feel the tangible pull of ending my life, the sweet relief. The peace. It is like returning to a favourite daydream, but it makes the tears spill over. For someone who never cried as a child, I seem to be finding it very easy to do so at the moment. It is not just tears rolling, it is deep crying that stops my breath and chokes me with mucus.

I know the process might not be peaceful, but the result would be peace – oblivion. It feels a bit clichéd to say 'at peace'. Is that what people would say? 'She is at peace now …'

Oblivion. I like the word. It is what I crave.

Monday 28 October 2002

Oceane

I decided to go to class today – yet in my head I had my mantra: 'It's OK – I will just kill myself.' Somewhere in me I am still hoping that something miraculous will happen to make me change my mind. Maybe I will meet someone or have a conversation or have a light-bulb moment that will change everything in the nick of time.

While thinking of suicide as my silver lining to a very big cloud, I have to consider the effect my planned actions will have. I picture my mum getting the phone call first, and then making calls to the rest of the family and friends. I say the words of the eulogies that will be spoken. And I cry their tears and mine.

I did have my reason for going to class today. I had biology lab and I wanted to get an extra blade for back-up. Remembering that moment of slipping the razor blade into my bag brings up the emotions again. They sit heavy in my gut and seem to surge out of me when I am in the safety of my room at the end of the day: 'I hate you I hate you I hate you.'

And now I've cut myself – three times in quick succession – on my arm. Just testing out the new blade and releasing some of my grief. I don't feel like I am a 'cutter' crying out for attention. I just feel so very angry at myself. That, and also I feel an intense sadness inside that I cannot express, and somehow by opening up a wound on my skin I am letting the pain show on the outside. Just a little bit.

Part of my hopelessness tonight is that the appointment with the psychiatrist this afternoon was not good at all. I should not have expected it to go differently, but part of me was hoping it might be the 'miracle' moment I was looking for. I sat and told her that all week since being on Zoloft I had felt worse. Nauseous, dissociated and unable to sleep. I tried to tell her this isn't the solution for me; the drugs are making me feel more helpless. I didn't go to the community mental health centre just to be put on medication. I couldn't quite express it clearly enough, and I got the impression that she was thinking, 'Mmm, you don't know what is best for you – you are crazy, I am sane, let me make the decisions.'

I wanted her to understand that taking pills suggests there is just some minor imbalance in my body. Something simple – that a few drugs can cure. Whereas it feels so much more than that to me. I need someone to say, 'Oh my God, of course you are feeling this way, this is HUGE. No, of course a pill won't fix it – we need to take more action – here, I have a plan.' And yet. Part of me knows that even if someone came up with the best plan in the world it would be too late. I have a sense deep in me that it is inevitable that I die. It is just the way it has to be.

I feel sorry for the psychiatrist, and the case manager assigned to me. I know they are following the correct protocol. Asking me the questions from their checklist. I know all the tricks though – answering their questions is a way to appease their worries or at least let them think I am safe. If I say how I truly feel, they will force me into a psychiatric hospital and involuntary treatment – drugs I am sure – all in the name of protecting me. I know that that is the worst possible solution for me. I would truly rather die than be locked up in a soulless place filled with crazy people. I know that I probably meet the criteria of being a crazy person, but I cannot bear the thought of being in a hospital, even more isolated, embarrassed and therefore just angrier at myself. No more shame. No more embarrassment. I want them to offer me another option, but they have not given me any hope of that today. I feel sly that I managed to con them into giving me three Temazepam tablets. Part of me wonders whether it is worth hanging on another week so that I can get three more. How many of these little sleeping pills would I need? Not sure I can wait.

I do feel like I am at the beginning of the end and that it is a one-way spiral down now. I am calmer – the brief cutting soothed me but more importantly, I know what I am going to do. There was no miracle today. I feel that the psychiatrist's dismissal of my side effects and seemingly flippant increase of the dosage was a sign that I am right – it is a hopeless situation. Drugs won't change what is going on. My racing heart when I hear footsteps approaching my door. My constant shame. My loneliness and feeling like a fraud around others. I'll always be like this while I am in this situation, and there is no point in them just increasing the drugs each week when I say I am still miserable. This year, the assault and all that it brought up has erased the parts of my life that were happy, the times that sustained me through the rough. I can no longer picture the freedom and exaltation of horseriding as a kid, of walking to the waterfall near our house for overnight adventures with marshmallows and bread cooked on the open fire.

Somehow my decision makes me feel safe. I don't have to worry about how I will cope with the side effects of the antidepressants. I don't have to worry about seeing Seth ever again. I don't have to worry about the fact that I feel broken and ruined. I don't have to worry about my body having been violated. I don't have to worry about having friends or feeling lonely. I don't even have to worry about the exams at the end of the year. I am going to kill myself. I know I will hurt some people terribly, but I will finally end this pain that has lurked throughout my life and now cascades uncontrollably.

Tuesday 29 October 2002

Oceane

Moving to college at the start of the year was meant to be my fresh start – independent, free from the weight of my family and the painful memories they brought. I was meant to be stepping into adulthood but instead, a few months in, Seth came and made me feel like no matter what I did, I would never find safety and security in my life. He proved, once again, that my body was not my own. That I would never lose my shame or the rotten ugliness in me. So, maybe it is weak of me. Cowardly. But I don't care. I am giving up.

Today I am still going through the motions of life: replying to emails, eating three meals. I even went to class again, to make it feel normal. Tonight is the night. No earlier than 6 pm, because I know Angie is on tutoring duty; she's on guard around me and will be worried if she doesn't see me at dinner. Sometimes I don't know if she is a friend or just doing her job as Duty Officer and Block Tutor. At 6 pm tomorrow, I am expected at a meeting at college for the duty officers, and I know people will come look for me if I don't show up. So between 6 pm tonight and 6 pm tomorrow is my chance.

I think of the relief some people will feel that I am dead. 'She was such a burden.' 'All that time wanting to talk.' 'Boring.' I wonder if Angie, who told me on Sunday that she needs a break from being my support to focus on her final exams, will feel relieved or guilty. When I reported to her back in March what Seth had done to me, she was so sweet and kind. But I've felt her pull back and I sense she has become sick of my tears and darkness.

My last hours feel intensely brief. There is all of a sudden so much I want to say. Whatever I write will be the last words I'll ever express to the world.

Sentences flash through my mind. Explanations. People I want to thank or apologise to. Some are the usual, closer friends. Others seem to leap into my mind unexpectedly. The people I lived with for a year during year 12 – why does it matter to me that they know I thought of them in my last hours on earth? I want to thank them and make sure that they know this isn't their fault. It is me who is weak, rotten inside, undeserving of life, ugly, unlovable, broken. Whatever I write feels inadequate and horribly naff and clichéd. I have scrunched up and thrown out a few versions – will people find these in the trash and read them too?

Suddenly my decision feels real and I am petrified. Do I have the strength to cut down to the veins in my arm?

Will I chicken out and be left with horrible scars that I won't be able to cover with a bracelet? It's OK, I have sleeping tablets, I have forty-eight Panadol. And some Panadeine – a full twenty-four pack. Maybe I could do something to make sure that I don't wake up from the drugged state I'll be in. A plastic bag over my head. I can remember my parents giving the boys and me a lecture on the potential for fatality of plastic bags over heads, after they saw one of us goofing around with one. I have options and plan B's, which makes me feel better. But at the same time, I wish so badly that I had another choice – some other way out of this. I feel so overwhelmed with the gravity of my decision. I can have rational thoughts but deep inside, I just feel so sad and so angry at myself. I'm crying again. I know what is coming. I can visualise myself slipping away.

Excerpts from suicide note

Nobody can see where I am.

Nobody can understand what I do.

Nobody can feel what I am going through.

I'm sorry that I couldn't be the fighter that you

wanted me to be

And that I wanted me to be too.

In this place I am all alone

I don't have your god always inside. There's just me.

By myself.

What is around the corner I'll never know, if I could get up and look it might be worthwhile, but I'd have to make that trip alone.

I'm lost in the void of darkness that is my life.
I want to be carried to the nothingness of my death.
Swallowed into emptiness.

Mother,
I don't know what I can say to stop the hurt I'm going to cause you. Please know that there's nothing you could do. I know how much you love me, please know how much I love you.

[*rest of note destroyed*]

Email from Oceane to Cécile, morning
They want to increase my medication to 100 mg per day. I am not too happy, but apparently that's the normal dose. What do you think?

It's sweet of you to offer to be in France while I travel in Europe, but I'll be fine. I have plenty of contacts there that I can call on if necessary – and we can stay on email contact.

Email from Cécile to Oceane, evening
Oceanette, got your last email. How are you going? Such pressure to study … Last lap, I hope you manage

your energy. About the 100 mg, it seems quite a lot.
I am used to people being given 50 mg. But then if
you are very depressed … it depends how you feel on
the 50 mg. Does it hold your head above the water? It
also depends … Have you had one breakdown or been
deeply depressed for a long time?

Did you actually make an appointment with that
psychiatrist guy I suggested to you to discuss all that?

How did you cope with the heat today? Did it
cool down at night? Also let me know about the food
situation … Do you want more patties, or something
else? Depending whether you want to come on Friday
night, I could either bring fresh stuff to you or have some
ready for you here.

Please let me know how you are. If you need to
defer because you cannot run the last lap, do not worry.
Your mental health is more important in the end …
OK, Dookie? Look after yourself and accept help …

BIG HUG, your Mumsk.

Cécile

The frogs are calling to each other in the dark outside
my windows. Where are you, Oceanette? No reply to my
email or to my calls. You've become silent. Why? Since
you told me that the local community mental health
centre was called after you had 'broken down' and has put
you on antidepressants, we've been in touch once or even

twice a day. I know how you hate taking the medication: it makes you feel nauseous and blurs your vision to the point that you cannot read or study.

I have tried to reassure you that medication is like an emergency rope to pull you out of the ditch when you don't have the strength to climb.

I've been checking my emails through the night. Nothing. Silence. Waiting is getting unbearable but I know that too much contact might feel like an intrusion. I am worried about you though, Oceanette, my darling.

Can't you call? Why don't you? Is it your need to feel independent? Are you trying to stay focused on your exams? Do you need space?

Wednesday 30 October 2002

Cécile

I am getting more frantic, checking my emails every hour or so. I have never done that before. I keep trying to reassure myself. I am just overanxious – that's what my friends have been telling me. So I admonish myself: She is a big girl. Leave her alone. She has to live her own life. Do not hassle her with your 'maternal anxiety'.

Excerpt from hospital notes

30/10/2002, 8 pm (acute mental health assessment)
18yo female known to Community Mental Health Centre team (referred to service ~2 wks ago). Assessed prior to being seen by M.O. Brought to A&E by uni friend/ support person, Bonnie.

Multiple attempts at suicide over the last 24 hours.

Difficult to assess as quite drowsy & physically sick (vomiting). Friend assisted by filling in the missing details.

Admits to having cut herself superficially on Sunday afternoon after having a stressful day. Did not need medical attention & stated it was not an attempt at suicide but rather an attempt to relieve tension. Again cut herself on Monday for the same purpose.

Mood deteriorated on Tuesday and Tuesday evening Oceane admits to having taken 48x panadol & 24x panadeine. She then cut both her wrists quite deeply & took 3x 10mg temazepam with the intention of falling asleep & not waking up. This was unsuccessful as she later woke up. She then put a bag over her head & reportedly fell asleep. She later woke up, took additional 48 panadol & attempted to strangle herself with the cord from her night gown. This was unsuccessful but she fainted upon standing up.

Oceane rang Bonnie (support person/friend) as she was resigned to the fact that she had been unsuccessful in her attempts. Bonnie then contacted her own father, who brought them to A&E. Oceane initially denied having taken any tablets but later during the assessment admitted to having taken the paracetamol O.D.

Appearance/Behaviour

Casually dressed female of stated age. Blood stained sleeves due to cut wrists. Vomiting throughout interview. Drowsy & difficult to assess. Pale.

Speech

Slowed. Minimal.

Mood

Depressed. Wishes she was successful in killing herself.

Affect

Depressed, flat.

Plan

To stay in A&E until medically clear – if attempts to leave, SII to be written & patient to be transferred to psychiatrist hospital nearby (bed booked).

If kept in overnight, patient to be r/v'ed in A.M. by acute team.

When medically clear, transfer to psychiatric hospital.

Acute team to contact Bonnie to offer support in A.M. Counselled briefly this evening, but is quite distressed after finding Oceane in blood stained bed. Would appreciate support tomorrow.

Thursday 31 October 2002

Cécile

Nothing from you again. By now, the anxiety has flooded my entire mind.

Still stopping myself from taking action. Several friends happen to call me in the evening on some totally unrelated matters. When they casually enquire how I am, I find myself invariably replying, according to the degree of closeness:

'I am so worried about Oceane,' or, 'I am so worried about my daughter.'

'What's wrong?'

'She has been very stressed and down.'

'Oh, but remember she always gets through … remember her last year of school, she nearly drove herself into the ground, didn't she? But she made it! She just drives herself so hard all the time!'

'We too easily take on our children's anxiety, don't we?'

'It's so hard to be a parent. We so much feel all their ups and downs. She'll be OK.'

Today, though, as there is no reply on your room phone number, or mobile, the thought crosses my mind: *What if she is dead in her room?* I immediately change it to a more reassuring one: *Maybe she is staying with one of her friends.* You have told me that you have good friends who are keeping an eye on you.

By night, I am frantic. Tossing and turning as I lie on my futon, checking my mobile and calling yours at an insane frequency. Still awake in the middle of the night, a vision appears of you being rocked very gently in some sort of canvas sling held by four elder women who appear to be your carers. Only then do I manage to get to sleep for a couple of hours.

Friday 1 November 2002

Cécile

Six am. Oceane, still no sign of you. I cannot bear this anymore. I have to find you. I am beyond the fear of intruding on your privacy.

I decide to call community mental health as soon as their office opens, to let them know how worried I am about you. I am told by the receptionist that no one can talk to me right now as all the workers are in a meeting that will finish at 9.30 am.

'Leave your name and phone number with me and someone will call you back as soon as the meeting is finished.'

It's 9.35 am. No call yet.

I call again and get onto a health worker, not your caseworker:

'I am very worried about my daughter who is under your care.'

'What's her name?'

'Oceane.'

'Oceane ... oh yes, just a minute ...'

Someone who knows about you, good: I was dreading being sent from one person to another.

'She is in hospital. Didn't you know?'

My blood chills.

'What? What's happened?'

'She's tried to kill herself … she is in hospital … I am sorry.'

At these words my world is turned upside down.

Oh no, not Oceane, not my child, not my own child, my beautiful daughter. No. No. No.

My mind crashes under tumbling images. My dearest sister Odile, thirty years old, lying dead on her bed after having put herself to sleep with a potent mix of pills – she was a doctor; she knew what to swallow. My little brother on the brink of adulthood, found by chance just in time with his wrists slashed and his stomach full of the contents of the bathroom cabinet. He was not a doctor; he did not know what to take. My eldest sister, hospitalised a number of times after attempts to end her life and her brain shattered by the quantity of electroshocks administered. My next sister, drugged silly and awfully scarred after setting herself on fire – 'an accident', they said. And even myself, at times touch and go – I have been vulnerable too.

No, not again, not in this family, not in my little family here. I ran away from France and my family – as far as I possibly could – to escape. So that this would not happen to my own child.

'Is she going to be OK?'

As if one could ever be OK after trying to kill oneself.

'She is in intensive care.'

Too many questions jumbled in my head. I need some time but I do not want the person to go.

'When did it happen?'

'She's been in hospital since Wednesday.'

'Since Wednesday? All that time. In intensive care – and nobody has called me!'

Images flash through my mind – you pale in a hospital room with monitors and tubes.

'Sorry,' says the community mental health worker. 'They should have called you. Why don't you ring the hospital?'

I jot down 'hospital – intensive care – Oceane' in case I blank and do not even remember your name.

The woman seems to realise that I am in shock. 'I'll give you the hospital number.'

I cannot get myself to ask more about what state you are in. Whether you are going to live. I am too scared.

I immediately press the digits for the hospital. I do not know if I'll be able to hold back the tears enough to speak. What do I need to ask? What will get me to you?

Every word is a huge effort:

'My name is Cécile, my daughter is in intensive care at your hospital, and I wonder if it is possible to talk to her or to somebody there.'

The person at the end of the line sounds so casual. *My daughter is in intensive care, how can you be so nonchalant?*

'I'll put you through, stay on the line.'

The waiting music comes on, unbearably irritating today.

'Hello, Intensive Care, Wendy speaking.'

Courage, Cécile, be strong, do not break down; it might stop you getting through to someone who can tell you about Oceane.

'Hello, my name is Cécile; I am the mother of Oceane, who is on your ward. I just want to find out how she is.'

'Oceane … who are you?'

'I am her mother.'

'Oh, would you like to talk to her?'

The images in my head shift: so you are conscious, you can talk on the phone. It gives me a bit of courage.

'Yes, please.'

I cannot believe my luck, and at the same time I am terrified of our first contact. There is no preparation for such moments. I try to calm myself by breathing attentively and slowly.

'Just a minute,' the voice continues. A few strange clickety sounds and there is your voice, weak, flat, tentative.

'Hello …'

Oceane

I feel paper thin. Translucent. I hurt, but I can't tell where the physical hurt stops and where the emotional hurt starts.

'Oceanette, chérie.'

When I hear your quiet, nearly whispering voice, I actually feel like I might vomit. I don't know who I thought would be on the phone, yet somehow, I am also not surprised it's you.

I can feel the tears pricking my eyes but I am so exhausted, I am scared of the abyss that tears might send me down.

Cécile

The utter pleasure – and utter pain – of the moment I hear your voice. You, alive. Yes, it is your voice on that phone line. I recognise it and yet I am not sure who you are anymore.

'Oceane, what's happened?' I say as softly as I can.

'How did you find out?'

You can put words together.

You say you are waiting for surgery on your hands.

'You've damaged things?'

'A bit.'

Sounds so simple, almost matter-of-fact.

Oceane

You ask me what has happened. How do I answer that? What has happened?

Instead I say, 'How did you find out?' By which I mean, How do I get out of this? What do I do now, Cécile?

I can mechanically tell you about the surgery I am waiting for – somehow it is the easiest thing to talk about. And part of me also wants you to know that this wasn't a half-hearted attempt. I am embarrassed that I failed – in the same way that I would be embarrassed if I failed a subject or got chastised for doing a bad job at work.

You speak again – and it is the quietness of your voice that undoes me. You want to come and see me. I don't know how to tell you that I can't cope with that.

As good as it is to hear a familiar loving voice, I can't cope with your sadness. It is what I was trying to say in my suicide notes: The thought of the grief my dying would cause you doesn't counterbalance my grief at living. It just adds to it, turns into my own grief. That's why your love is not enough to make me live – I can't feel it anymore, Cécile. I can only add your sadness to my own.

I have spent so much of my life protecting you, doing what was necessary to shelter you. I can't tolerate your needs now. I can feel the pain that I am causing by saying 'no'. I tell you that you could come visit after the surgery maybe – I wonder if I will make it that long; I would prefer to slip into death before facing the pain I have caused you and everyone else. Inside I am willing my liver to give up – 'I am not worth it,' I want to tell it.

I think back to you, crying and falling apart, when I was seven or eight years old. I am angry that I had to witness your sadness. I was the child, you were the mother – but that's not how it felt, Cécile. I need you to accept that my needs are not aligned with your needs. You need to visit me, I can feel it in your voice. But the only strength I have is from my independence, and that will be devalued if I admit to needing you.

'Oceane, I so much want to see you, you know – just to be with you. Please, can I?'

'No. I'll call you tomorrow.'

I hand the phone back to the nurse, who is looking at me curiously – I am not sure if I detect sympathy in her eyes.

Cécile

Your 'no' falls like a guillotine. Is it a 'no' I need to respect in order to save our connection, the connection that got so battered after I split up from your dad – or is it a 'no' I need to trespass?

Ten minutes later, I call you again.

'Oceane, what do I tell your brothers? Remember, Leon is arriving from France tomorrow night. Julian and I are going to the airport.'

'I DON'T WANT Leon to know!'

You are so clear, as if you have thought about it already. You have not been close for a number of years – it makes sense.

'You can tell Julian. Just tell him I had an accident and that I am in hospital and he can call me. And above all' – your voice becomes intense – 'under no circumstances do I want Oliver to know.'

Why such insistence on your dad not knowing anything?

'One thing you could do for me,' you add, 'is call Annemaree. You can tell her what happened. Ask her if she could get in touch with the people who are going to take Freya and tell them that I have had an accident and won't be able to do anything for a while.'

Such a relief to be able to help, to call our friend Annemaree about your horse. Even to know that your horse is on your mind. You are still caring for her. Does it mean you want to live?

'Sure, I'll do that.'

How do I say goodbye to my daughter whose survival is only a hope and who seems to be determined to endure her ordeal by herself?

I sit there on the floor of my office, phone handset limp in my hand. I close my eyes and breathe slowly, waiting for my brain to tick again. There are no thoughts, no words, no feelings, just breathing carefully, just waiting for something to emerge in my head or in my guts. Just something.

Oceane

My body feels like it is floating above the bed. It is like a million-year-old skeleton, still together in the correct form, but a puff of air will make it disintegrate into powder. The pain in my arms is what scares me the most. I need a way out but without suffering any more physical pain. I am even more desperate still for death; it's teasing me with how close it is. More so than ever, I am terrified of failing to die. I can't bear to live with the consequences of what I've done.

If I thought that I felt lonely before my attempt, then it barely holds a candle to how I feel now in hospital.

I am angry at myself for weakening and finally admitting to all the painkillers I took – even the second pack of forty-eight Panadol. Maybe if I hadn't said anything my liver would have failed and let me slip away while they were focused on the blood loss and strangulation. I don't know why I told them – I think I knew the game was up, that I had failed and that I might as well cooperate now. I think it was also the pain in my gut, the acrid taste of the tiny amounts I was vomiting every few minutes.

In truth, it was probably my stubborn pride also. I needed the doctor to know that I meant it. I could tell in the way he spoke to me, after I'd been taken through emergency, that he didn't think I deserved to live. And I wasn't going to argue with him. I remember thinking to myself as he sneered at my wrists and the damage I'd done: *I wonder if he hates me enough to help me finish the job?* I knew he thought I was a waste of space and time and there were people who didn't do such things to themselves that deserved treatment over me.

They asked me if I was pregnant and then told me they had to do a pregnancy test anyway, despite my clearly saying no. They asked me whether I had taken any other drugs, but then took the blood to test for them anyway. I think I would have preferred them not to ask rather than pointedly indicate they didn't believe me. Once again, it's like my body isn't mine – but this time it's the doctors and nurses stripping me of my autonomy.

It was strange in the emergency section, watching them call around for available liver donors that might be a match for my blood. The doctors would lean on the counter, glancing at me as they described the situation in medical terms.

'We have a young female, eighteen years, high lethality suicide attempt with multiple deep lacerations to her forearms and ingestion of approximately ninety-six Paracetamol and an additional twenty-four Panadeine, three Temazepams. Blood tests to confirm other drugs. Blood type O Rhesus positive. She is not stable yet, but we have her on par-??? and ??? blah blah milligrams of mumble mumble.'

I remember being pressured to tell my family, and somehow it felt safer to call my ex-stepmother, Miranda, than Cécile. Seeing her shock and distress when she arrived was like a practice run for what I was going to have to face eventually with Cécile.

I am racking my brain for plans that will definitely work. Climbing up an electric pole and electrocuting myself? Can't climb with my arms like this. Jumping off a cliff? Somehow jumping is too violent for me. I need something gentle for my poor hurting body. More pills? Eurgh, I feel sick just thinking about it – I don't even know how I could swallow one pill, my stomach is so tender. Starve myself to death? Maybe. How could I hide it from everyone for long enough? Would it hurt? Drown? How do you make yourself stay under water when you start struggling for air? Car exhaust? Definitely happy with the idea of just slowly falling asleep. I don't have a car though. Would someone lend me a car?

The lady from the acute team at the community mental health centre came back again this afternoon. It is the same questions again. Asking how I am medically. Asking how I am feeling. Asking if I am still suicidal. She told me that she'd come yesterday – I have no memory of that, only the visit from my friends. I must have been so far away.

I answered with my cheeriest smile and the most positive energy I could muster. Part of me nearly believes that I feel this good – but not quite. I hate being deceitful but I know that I have to get out of here. I have been moved from emergency to ICU, and it is deadening. I am the only person under eighty years old, and I feel like I am on display in the centre of the ward. No privacy curtains pulled around. Everyone staring at the huge elbow-high bandages and endless cords and machines around me.

The lady asked me about something, and my response was a bit blasé; I said I was looking forward to leaving hospital after my surgery. She just looked at me and suggested it would take longer than that to 'sort things out'.

Cécile

I know I need to call Annemaree about your horse, but first I want to speak to the person called Bonnie, the friend who took you to the hospital. I can't even remember the name of your college. I get the phone book, look for the university – that name I can recall – and luckily the word 'residences' pops out in bold.

'Hi, my name is Cécile Barral. Can I talk to Bonnie?'

A voice comes on.

'Bonnie speaking.'

'Oh, hello, I am Oceane's mum. I just found out what's happened. Can you tell me something?'

The person called Bonnie says something happened on the weekend that was the final straw. She also talks of the fighting at home, of you not feeling safe, even in your own family that loves you.

There is a pause.

'Does Oceane actually know you are talking to me?'

'No. I just do not know what to do. Do you think it is all right for me to go and see her? I thought you might have a sense.'

'Oceane needs to know you've called me, I have to tell her.'

'I'd rather tell her myself,' I just manage to slip in before Bonnie closes the door completely.

So, Oceane, here I am, calling you again at the risk of annoying you or interrupting your rest. But in the last fifteen minutes, my world has turned upside down. So many questions, decisions.

And also, just hearing your voice is a reassurance that you are still there. I'd like to be at the end of the line with you all the time.

This time, getting to you over the phone is so easy, already a routine.

'Oceane, chérie, I am sorry to call you again. I just need to tell you, I just called Bonnie.'

You want to know every detail of what has been said between Bonnie and me. The keenness gives life to your voice. I ask you again if I can come.

'No. I promise I will call you after the surgery.'

Next I call my friend and colleague Maggie, who is horrified and understands I cannot talk more, and yes, I do not need to worry, she will cancel all my appointments.

I trust her with this: she knows our family and she also will know how to be sensitive when calling my clients. We agree that she will tell my clients that one of my children has just had an accident, is OK, but that I need to attend to the child; I will be away for two weeks; they can call her if they need to and she will keep them informed if anything changes in the meantime.

As I go to the kitchen to put the phone down, I pick up a message of cancellation via our work voicemail for David, the colleague that I have shared a practice with for many years. I call him to pass on the message. Funny how keeping obligations gives me some self-pride. I burst into tears.

'What's wrong?'

I tell him what's happened and how I so much want to go and see you but how you've refused.

'You have to go! You are her mother,' he says simply, in his firm voice.

I eventually reach Annemaree on her mobile. She isn't home in the Mountains, but is having lunch in a noisy City cafe. I tell her about you and manage not to forget to pass on your message about your beloved horse.

She too says without any hesitation, 'Cécile, go! Of course, you want to be with her. Go, Cécile, go!'

After pacing the house, in tears, disoriented, I decide I have to leave. Home is not home right now, not the place of comfort it normally is. The little tasks I usually do have lost all meaning.

I'll start driving to the hospital, just start driving, and if on the way I come to realise I am doing the wrong thing, then I can always turn around. If I make it to the hospital, I'll go to the ICU door and ask if I can see you. I imagine a nurse passing her head through the door of your room and asking in a nice friendly nurse-like manner: 'Your mum is here, would you like to see her?'

I just have to brace myself for the possibility of your refusal. So be it. At least you'll know that I wanted to be with you.

The need to concentrate on driving combined with the lulling of the car engine on the highway seems to help a bit. I float through the traffic. Luckily the way is familiar enough. The landscapes seem strangely new, though.

The hospital feels very inhospitable – a puzzle of higgledy-piggledy old, dark, dirty brick buildings connected by more recent passageways. It seems every vacant bit has been patched with a newer building.

I follow the signs to the ICU and come to the desk. A young nurse appears. I muster all my strength, especially in my throat and diaphragm, to utter words without breaking into sobbing.

'Can I see Oceane? I am her mum.'

The nurse disappears without further enquiry.

A minute later, she reappears. 'Come with me.'

I think she is taking me to a room, probably a shared room.

'Here she is.' The nurse points to a bed.

Here you are.

You lie half-reclined, white gowned; only the tips of a few iodine-smeared, lifeless fingers are visible below the thick fresh bandages wrapped around both your forearms and hands. Your hair is plaited like a little girl's, but without the shine little girls' plaits normally have. Your face is pale and not much life is left in your eyes. The ward is packed; you are by far the youngest: spotless, innocent in the middle of the other beds occupied by spluttering, muttering, old people.

Your bed has been rolled right into the middle of the ward, so visible, as if the staff want to expose you or maybe make sure you are seen at all times, just in case.

When you recognise me, your face seems to drop, your eyes look down before you timidly look at me.

The pain wrenches my heart and throat. I lean over and kiss you on your forehead, holding back the tears that swell up. I am sure you do not need an upset mother.

'Oceane, I am so glad you are alive!' I say in a quiet voice.

You look down. Maybe you are not glad. You slowly move your head from one side to the other, letting me know you wish you had died.

At that moment, our wishes are worlds apart.

I sit on the chair by your bedside. You look so fragile.

41

No questions, Cécile, gentle talking only, no investigative look.

But I still ask: 'Are you in pain? Have you been able to sleep? When is the surgery due?'

You give me bits of information, in a flat, slow voice interspersed with silences.

They are waiting for your liver functions to pick up to transfer you to another hospital for surgery. They have stitched the right wrist, but not the left one – the one with more damage to it – where they are going to try to do repair work on your tendons and nerves. You have no feeling in your left thumb and forefinger. They haven't given you anything for pain relief.

'How come?'

'Because of my liver,' you say. Leaving me to guess what may have happened.

My brain throbs silently – what happened, what happened? How could you do so much violence to yourself?

You explain how they had you ready for a liver transplant. You tell me the registrar had come to your bed and said: 'You know, you are going to die.' Trying to shock you back into life? Or angry at another young life wasted?

But at the last minute the drug they had given you to get your liver to work (although they did not have much hope) had started to kick in and your liver had started to respond, like a broken clock that you shake.

When I first talked to you on the phone, I realise, the liver drug had not yet kicked in, you were still hoping to die and you did not want me or anyone there to know. Such strength in your determination and secrecy, and such utter aloneness too.

Your dear old liver would not let you get rid of yourself.

A nurse drops a dinner tray on the table by the side of your bed and swivels it so the food is over your immobilised hands, literally under your nose. No word, not even any eye contact. You look at the food in disgust; you will not let me help you eat.

I ask, 'Do you remember that day you asked me if I had regrets? And I answered, "No, not really, because even what went wrong I feel I have learnt from." Now, you know, I do have regrets ...'

Tears choke my throat as you raise your eyes towards me.

'I regret I haven't been able to protect you.'

Your eyes well up with your own tears: a brief moment of intimacy.

Then another nurse comes to say that there is a bed for you at another hospital and that the ambulance will be here very soon.

You want to see me after the surgery. You seem to believe that after the surgery, everything will be fine, back to normal. As if there will be no trace of your killing yourself.

You let me pack your bag of clothes and a few small belongings. I am so happy to be able to do a little something for you. The bag is unfamiliar, pink flowery padded cotton – not my style. My heart pinches: the bag would have been brought here by Miranda, your ex-stepmother. Closer in age to you than to your dad. You've let her in.

I focus a bit longer than necessary on opening the zip of the bag so as to keep behind my eyeballs the wave of rage and tears that is swelling up.

You look exhausted and it is time for me to leave. I am acutely aware that I am forcing my presence on you.

Oceane, my darling, I love you, I just love you, that's all, and I have never stopped loving you, you know. I'll do anything to help. Will you ever have a chance to know that?

'I'll go now, chérie, the ambulance should be here soon.' *Is this my final goodbye*, I wonder, as I place a tender kiss on your forehead. Although every bit of my energy is used up holding this body of mine together, I manage: 'I'll see you tomorrow.'

You avert your gaze. If only I could be reassured that there will be a tomorrow, that you will make it through surgery. *Will you make it, Oceanette? It might be so easy to let yourself slip away.*

You have told me they might not be able to give you a general anaesthetic because of your liver, and my brain cannot fathom the implications. 'When they work on you, don't look,' I say as I leave. 'Try to make nice pictures in your mind.'

So, I leave you on that Friday late afternoon.

My body walks away through the swinging doors, down a poorly lit hallway in which I bump into Annemaree, who instead of returning home to the Mountains after lunch has come to find you.

'Cécile!' She gives me a hug that holds all the pain, fear, hope, disbelief, the lot.

'You go in, Annemaree, the ambulance is arriving soon.'

She looks into my eyes: 'Wait for me, Cécile. We'll have a cup of tea together after I've seen Oceane.'

Does she realise how much it means to me, not having to walk out of this place totally alone? I am so grateful to have someone here who is special to both of us. You and Annemaree share a love of horses, and your regular rides together gave you an escape during difficult times. Meanwhile, she and I have shared long walks in the Mountains, along with the ups and downs of our lives.

I wait and think about a time a few months ago, when I was telling friends how I was going to Vietnam because at last, after so many challenges, all my children were well. Julian was settled in a shared City flat and working in hospitality as he'd always wanted. Leon was taking time to travel before starting uni. I believed your main stress was from studying too hard. I thought that as soon as you flew off to Europe for the summer vacation you had planned, you would feel free and light.

Twenty minutes later Annemaree joins me in the hospital cafeteria.

'I managed to feed her a bit!'

I know she means to convey something positive and hopeful, but my heart hurts. You can take food from Annemaree, not from me. But in the end all that really matters is that you have taken in some nourishment.

Oceane

I have been in hospital for three days but my normal relationship to time has disappeared. It feels like both three hours and three weeks.

Cécile came to the hospital anyway, despite my half-dozen times of saying, 'No, I don't want you to come.' When I saw her arrive I felt the same weight pressing down on me as I had when I heard her voice on the phone, but really I have no idea whether I am glad or angry. Having visitors the last few days has been enlivening. The saving grace of having Cécile visit was that straight after, Annemaree also came and that made it feel safer. Annemaree brought sweet dates and fed them to me, which was strange. I felt both nourished and awkward at being fed like a baby.

There are certain friends I am able to get a sense of support from. Somehow their emotions do not weigh on me so heavily. Despite being fairly new friends from college, Ben, Dina and Alice came to see me. Ben and Dina are nearly like twins, both blond and shy, whereas Alice's height and confidence gives her a louder presence. They made me feel good, unlike the creeping shame I get when I think of Bonnie and Angie, and what they must think of me now. Yesterday with Ben, Dina and Alice, I felt more present and could laugh more than I have all year, even though the memory feels already foggy and distant today. I have such a desperate need to be seen and acknowledged by others, so I am not sure why I am pushing Cécile away so strongly. I feel allergic to her, like she is taking from me – whereas my friends' visit gave me a genuine sense of aliveness.

I was also rescued from the stress of Cécile's visit by a call from the hospital where they want to operate, to say they had the bed ready for me. My first ambulance trip but I feel only nervous anticipation of what will happen next.

At the new hospital I am left on the trolley for what seems to be a long, long time. I am still technically supposed to be 'nil-by-mouth' pending surgery, although I had the dates from Annemaree. My lips and mouth are so dry and uncomfortable.

I am finally taken into a consulting room, with a registrar. This one is a youngish male, and it feels like the same shit as with all the other psychiatrists, counsellors and psychologists who traipsed in and out at the first hospital. I am a bit cocky, partly from exhaustion and partly from being sick of these little games of questions. I feel like I am being judged, and it makes me self-conscious. By now I have worked out that there is a 'right' answer and a 'wrong' answer, and I play to it. I don't like being manipulative, but I also feel like they are testing me to see if I tell the same story each time.

This guy speaks impatiently, like he is already running late, and keeps going on about antidepressants. He seems to latch on to me saying that I felt odd on the Zoloft and that the side effects were so unhelpful. He indicates that a potential side effect of Zoloft is 'disinhibition and behaviours that could be redirected into violent suicide attempts'. Bingo! My new best story: Sorry, Mister Psychiatrist, it was just the side effects of Zoloft. If I can sell that one, it will be easier to convince them that I don't need to stay in hospital.

The registrar talks a lot about psych beds, and which psych hospital might be able to take me, which makes me extremely scared. I can't really allow myself to think about it because it overwhelms me; I have no tolerance for any strong emotion. I also resent being dragged into the sorry tale of hospital-bed availability. I'm sure the health system is a bit fucked, Mister, but not really my biggest problem right now, yeah? It is freaking me out to hear you list the names of psych wards and how they have no beds. Why can't you hear me saying I don't want a bed? I just want to be looked after at home. But you aren't listening, are you?

Finally I am settled into my own room, complete with my own full-time nurse to watch over me. Disconcerting, being watched, but as it took till after 11 pm to get me off the ambulance trolley and into a bed, I am too knackered to care very much.

Saturday 2 November 2002

Cécile

I wake at home in the Mountains and the pain hits me. My whole body is aching, especially my throat; I cannot move, I need somebody with me.

I leave messages on my friend Theresa's voicemail. God I hate that mechanical friendly voice: 'This is Telstra 101 message bank service for ...' I hope for some divine intervention that will make Theresa, who often does not answer her phone, pick up just this one time.

Oceane, I cannot move, not my body, even less my mind. Both refuse to cooperate.

After many failed attempts at reaching Theresa, I manage to take one step: I drive my frozen self to her place, only a couple of minutes away. It is as far as my body and my mind will go. As I pull into the car park at the back of her house, she is rushing to her own car. She sees me; her big eyes look at me enquiringly. I step out of my car. Looking at her is uncomfortable and yet I need her so much.

'Theresa!'

'Cécile, what's happening? I was just coming to your place. I've just heard the messages and gathered something must be wrong.'

I hug her as the sobs take over.

'Oceane tried to kill herself,' I blurt out.

'Oh, Cécile.' The same disbelief as everyone.

Oceane, no one could imagine you turning against yourself like that. We all have the image of the solid, determined, super-competent Oceane. It just does not fit.

Theresa drives home with me. We sit next to each other at the kitchen table facing the bush on this clear late spring day. It is still cool in the Mountains. There is nothing much to say and yet unformed words tumble all over my brain.

Theresa just puts her hand on my forearm. 'Oh, Cécile.'

After staring at the mountain for a while, the warmth of Theresa's hand brings me back. I go and get the emails you and I exchanged in the last couple of weeks and read them aloud to Theresa. Maybe they will help me understand something new? Now I am reading them in a different light. How could I have missed so much?

Thursday 17 October, 6.57 am: 'I am sorry I can't talk to you, it's nothing to do with you or anything but I just find it too "in-the-family" kind of thing. It's too emotionally difficult to talk or tell you things because I know you love me. And I know how you feel, and from somebody who cares about me like my mother, it's kind of too much. I feel fairly stuck at the moment, all my options are too difficult, I just need to make it to the end of term and then I can try and find a way to get help. It just seems like such a long way away.'

All there, how could I have missed it?

Thursday 17 October, 7.26 pm: 'Pouchkine, of course I worry; that's part and parcel of being a parent. I just hope you recognise when you are pushing your limits too much or when the pain is too much and do what you need to do to get help. You deserve it. If I can help, tell me. Lots of love, your mama.'

Theresa helps me get Leon's room ready and leaves when I feel able to have a little rest before driving to the City.

Julian calls – he has figured out what has happened and decides he wants to join me at the hospital and then come with me to pick up Leon at the airport. I sense he wants, or needs, to play the big brother role. I am happy not to be alone but do not know how it is going to be for him to see you. We organise to meet in the hospital's foyer.

Then your father rings. He hasn't called me in years; we have led such opposite lives in the nearly six years since separating. After the bitter fighting back then, I have enjoyed that, with grown-up kids, I now rarely have to deal with him. I tell him you are alive, yes, you are in hospital and that I cannot talk more, I need to respect your wishes for privacy. In fact, he probably knows as much as I do, if not more, through Miranda. I just tell him that I am off to the hospital.

The fluidity of the Saturday traffic to the City is somewhat soothing. Each kilometre brings me closer to you. The nature of time has changed – it is not the usual kind, but a foreign version; at times so slow, at times so accelerated.

Oceane

My operation was cancelled this morning – put off until later today. Feel so weak and exhausted. Hard to think straight.

I get a new nurse every six hours or so. Some walk in and engage straight away. Others sit and read their magazine and barely say hello. One even got straight to the point and said, 'What did you go and do something so silly like that for?'

Cécile came back, with Julian. It was OK seeing Julian. But I couldn't engage in a conversation with him. I know he can guess why I am in hospital, but I can't face telling him officially. I want to (need to?) pretend it was just an accident. I wish it was – I wish that I'd just driven a car into a tree or something. Be so much easier to explain. Fewer questions; less embarrassment and dread about people's reactions. With Cécile, I can see her utter focus on me, but I also sense a disconnection. She is here against my wishes and requests, another boundary not respected.

I need her to convince someone to let me out of here. But I also need to pretend I don't need her.

The psychiatrist I saw today (a different one again) was very different to the others. She made it clear that I was not going anywhere. I hadn't realised that I was scheduled, not allowed to leave, could be held here against my will. Feels awful.

I sense Cécile is on my side or at least understands that I need to be out of hospital. That helps me cope with having her here.

Cécile and Julian left pretty early to go and pick up Leon from the airport. I desperately don't want Leon to know why I am here. After all he has put me through, I don't think he's earned the right to know something so personal about me.

Cécile

Julian is there, on time. It says a lot about how much he cares for you and wants to be there. I am so used to him promising something, only to change his mind at the last minute.

'Oceane – orthopaedic unit, room 42, fourth floor,' says the lady at the reception desk.

Lifts, corridors; orthopaedic unit: follow the signs. The nurses' station.

The anxiety tightens my stomach, a state of alertness. It could not be worse than yesterday. Or could it? Maybe

I am worried about more tubes and post-operative devices.

A nurse confirms room 42, and shows a door ajar just by the station.

I give a little knock and pass my head through the door.

'Hel...lo.' Only your eyes move as you catch sight of both our faces close together in the door. You are lying on your white bed like yesterday, only paler, weaker, and you are hooked to a drip to keep your fluids up.

'Hey Julian.' You both smile awkwardly, but are obviously pleased to see each other. You even manage to exchange bits of teenage cool chitchat. 'Howzit going? Pretty good' sort of stuff. Echoes of the Oceane we thought we had only a few days ago.

You look at me wearily: 'I haven't had the operation.'

'You are still waiting? How come?'

A blue nurse gets up from the armchair next to your bed, folds up a *Who* magazine and interrupts:

'Excuse me, are you going to be here for a while?'

'Yes,' I answer tentatively, not sure what her question is about.

'Do you mind if I go and have a break? But if you go, you have to tell the nurse at the station straight away.'

I realise you are on twenty-four-hour watch. You are a high-risk patient.

'Sure,' I say as normally as I can.

You continue: 'The surgeons were too busy with emergencies throughout the night.'

This is the reality of public health – not enough surgeons; money squeezed from health into more tax cuts for those who don't need it.

You haven't eaten or had any fluids since last night, except on the drip, because you'll be wheeled to the theatre as soon as they have a space. You look too fragile for me to even dare sit at the end of your bed – the sheets need to stay intact, bleached white. Not much we can do or say – you obviously need to conserve the little energy you have left. I stroke your forehead.

That evening, Julian and I leave you, both just wanting to cry, but each trying to keep strong for the other.

We end up in a cafe at the nearby railway station. We need food and drink to ground ourselves. Our day is not finished. We are both desperate for some comfort beyond what we can give each other, so we spend time on the phone to our respective friends. I can see Julian at the phone booth across from the station forum, off and on in tears. I still hold my own tears back. I cannot afford to go back to the mess I was in this morning, when I thought I would not be able to drive.

How is it going to be at the airport? Leon is going to realise straight away that something is terribly wrong. In the last two years, Julian and Leon have finally been on speaking terms after well over a decade of silence, but their relationship is still tentative. After probably no contact during Leon's year overseas, Leon wouldn't expect Julian there. He will notice the absence of joy; he might think we are not that happy to see him. We'll have to tell him. How? Who will give him the news? When?

Julian and I drive to the airport sad, heavy in our hearts, angry and frightened, but it does feel good to do this together.

Julian says, 'I will tell Leon.'

He wants to help, to take on the difficult task. Oceane, I am so full of conflicting feelings. I am so happy not to be alone to tell Leon about you. I also have whiffs of resentment at being robbed of the pleasure of hugging Leon joyfully after his year of travelling.

When the screens announce that Leon's plane has landed, Julian and I look at each other, terrified. We walk to the arrivals gate. The lights are harsh. Bunches of people have gathered waiting for their dear ones.

Will I recognise Leon? A year is a long time. Will he have long hair? Or short hair? Be tanned? Or pale? Bigger? Or thinner?

How are our eyes going to meet? Or not meet?

Julian rehearses various sentences, wavers, is tempted to pass the job on to me, ultimately stays determined: he wants to be the strong one.

A few backpackers of similar age to Leon pass through the gate and I am not even sure they are not Leon. After a while and many, many passengers, I think the plane must be empty and still no Leon. Then he appears, long-haired, soft, supple and free, with a bright snowboard bag loaded on a luggage trolley. My son is here, wholesome, unscathed. He looks wonderful.

'Leon!'

The joy, the pleasure – just for that instant.

Julian and I hug him in turn, but Julian's face becomes serious as he looks into Leon's eyes. Leon's joy immediately, almost imperceptibly tones down. His fluid muscles halt.

'Leon ...'

Leon's eyes become fixed. He looks at Julian, then at me. He has become unsettled, worried.

'What?'

Julian's words rush out, awkwardly: 'Leon, it's Oceane, she is OK, but she's in hospital, she's had a bad accident.'

Leon takes on the appearance of a wild animal. 'What? What?' He hits his head with his fist, as if to wake himself up to reality. 'What? Tell me, what happened?'

'Let's go and sit down,' says Julian, wisely. 'She is OK. She is in hospital.'

'Tell me, tell me now. What's happened?'

'Leon, she's tried to kill herself.'

Leon looks even wilder. He shakes his head.

'Oceane? No, that is not possible.'

Leon, too, the same response. No, not you ...

'Yes, Leon, she did. We are as shocked as you are. Let's go and sit, we'll tell you. We've just come from the hospital.'

By this stage, Leon is freefalling into our nightmare and has to sit. He keeps pushing his luggage trolley, with Julian and I on either side of him, each holding under one of his arms. The snowboard bag has lost its shine.

We sit at a table. Leon keeps shaking his head: 'Oceane, no! What, what's happened?'

'We don't know, Leon. She is in hospital. She is probably having an operation on her hands right now. She's cut the nerves and tendons on her wrists.'

Leon bursts into tears.

'Oceane! No, no, not Oceane.' As we tell Leon the only little bits we know, he listens, shaking his head in disbelief.

We explain to Leon how you do not want anyone to know. How I have found you by chance really.

'Can I see her tomorrow? I need to see her. Even if I cannot talk with her, I need to see her.'

'I understand, Leon; this is exactly how I felt yesterday. Of course, we'll all go together tomorrow.'

God, only yesterday.

Leon says how glad he is to be with us. How he would have had to jump on a plane anyway. How much worse it would be to be separated from us. We are together.

In silence, we drive out of the airport and through a few suburbs to Julian's shared flat; then Leon and I start the drive back home to the Mountains.

No sooner have we arrived home than Oliver is on the phone again. He wants to know exactly what has happened. I do not know what to tell him. I just want to protect you as much as possible.

Oceane, pouchkine, I wish I could understand. I am lost in the darkness of your silence.

Sunday 3 November 2002

Oceane

No surgery again last night. Feel exhausted. My mouth, lips, throat are burning. I am occasionally allowed to suck on an ice cube, but I just want a gulping drink of something cold.

Cécile came again, with Leon this time, followed by Julian soon after.

Cécile popped in first and asked if I wanted to see Leon. Not sure what she wanted me to say; it seems like it is no use saying 'no' to her, seeing she seems to go ahead anyway. I am trapped in my usual pattern: I want to say no to something, but I feel horrendous guilt and a sickening sense of hurting the person, so I say yes.

Leon comes in and he looks like a rabbit in headlights. All anxiety and wildness. I haven't seen him for ages; he has been travelling for at least a year. I am so relieved he doesn't stay long. I feel I have nothing I want to say to him, and trying to make him feel better only zaps me of energy I can't spare. All I can really think about is my hunger and thirst and whether my body will withstand this operation.

Do I want it to withstand it? Can I convince my body to slip away under anaesthetic?

Cécile

Leon and I arrive at the hospital early in case you accept to see him before Julian joins us.

You and Leon fell out during the year you shared a flat in the Capital. You were doing year 11, and he year 12; he had been kicked out of the boarding house he'd lived in the previous year.

Leon had supported your leaving Oliver and Miranda's house to attend school in the Capital. He had sensed you were deeply unhappy and needed to escape. I naively believed his promise to be your big brother and look after you. You were so young to move out of home. Not that Leon's extra fourteen months made him that much older than you.

'How come you are not moving too?' a social worker asked me over the phone. Your move out of home as a fifteen-year-old had been flagged in the system when you tried to apply for youth study allowance. I wish I could have moved with you. I explained to her how my only income was from my private psychotherapy practice I had slowly established and I could not just take a break. The Capital was too far to travel back and forth and I did not have the resources to fly. There was no choice – and I had numbed myself to the madness of this situation.

I told myself that you would be spending many weekends in the Mountains and I could come visit you too. And then there was your Oma and Grandpa, Miranda's parents, so loving and generous, who invited you for a homely meal every week. 'They are keeping a good eye on her,' is what I told myself. Survival mode made me so blind.

You did come home most weekends. On Saturdays I would help you clean the stables where your horse was kept – my way of helping with the cost of agisting Freya. It was also our time together, Oceanette. You would tell me of the troubles you had living with Leon, but as always, I thought you were coping better than you were. You refused to move out of your flat, despite the stress, because you had 'done nothing wrong' and I did not dare insist that Leon should leave. I sensed he was starting to go off the rails and I was terrified of losing him.

Once again you became the sacrificed one.

Today, the way to your hospital room is already familiar. This time the nurse leaves straight away, not even asking if I mind. She must have deemed me safe enough to look after you. I find you still waiting for surgery. They were not able to operate last night; too many emergencies. You haven't yet been able to eat or drink. You look even paler. How much longer can you wait?

I tell you that Leon so much wants to say hello. He has been gracious about your possible rejection of him. He understands, it's OK, he loves you all the same.

But yes, Leon can come in. The two of you chat: small talk, none of the real questions that he too is burning to ask.

Monday 4 November 2002

Oceane

Awful vomiting, sick feeling. I can barely open my eyes with the after-effects of the general anaesthetic.

I went in finally around midnight. It was strange having no one seeing me off before the operation. Bit like suicide; felt I was leaving without anyone knowing. Wheeled down the corridors by strange nurses. I was left in the pre-op room for half an hour.

Finally the blue-masked, gowned and hatted intern came with the chart, flopped it down onto my legs and said, 'So, Sally, you are here to have your appendix out?'

I wished I had someone holding my hand so that I could laugh with them about this huge stuff-up. It made me feel more vulnerable, but luckily they got the right chart, looking very embarrassed, and I was reassured that I would wake up with fixed arms and an appendix still in my body.

Apparently the surgery took over four hours as there was more nerve damage than they had thought. I get some satisfaction out of this. It lessens my embarrassment at my failure that at least my attempt was serious.

I barely remember waking in recovery. There is something very unique about the feeling general anaesthetic gives you. The blankness. I just remember the nausea and throwing up after and the desperate need to keep sleeping.

The doctor came in at 8.30 this morning. I was still asleep but they woke me up and did the usual rundown and two-minute examination. I have some sensations in my hands and wrists, which are now in heavy, thick casts. Before the operation I had a sense of tingling and numbness at the same time – a bit like constant dead arms. Now, they feel like they are balloons. I have an uncanny sense that they are swelling and deflating in exact rhythm with my breath. Like someone is blowing up a balloon and then sucking the air back out. If I hold my breath, the balloon sensation stops too. I feel completely drugged.

I think Leon and Cécile came – can't even remember if it was a dream or not.

I remember drinking juice and feeling the rawness of my throat after so long without liquid. I am fine with the first few sips but later, when I greedily gulp it, desperate to soothe my thirst, I vomit and vomit and vomit, until I am completely empty again.

I want the feeling of the general anaesthetic again. The sense that you are dead. I am in too much pain to even plan or think about killing myself right this minute; I just crave my own overdose of anaesthetic. So much less messy – so much less pain and fear than the way I did it. It would be perfect if I could convince someone to give me a general anaesthetic and kill me while I am gone. I am convinced it would be the humane thing to do – like for a suffering animal.

Cécile

As soon as Leon and I enter your room the nurse does her usual bolting number. We find you lying on your ultra clean bed, drips and tubes around, even whiter than the day before although that would seem impossible.

They have finally operated on you during the night. You look utterly powerless with both forearms and hands in thick fresh plaster casts, vivid iodine painted over your fingers – or, more exactly, the visible swollen tips of your fingers. Just above the line of the cast, three parallel scars, still raw and red – a remnant from your night of rampage?

You have to ask for every single little thing, you who hate asking. Yes, you would like me to get you some fresh juice from the deli at the railway plaza.

I leave Leon with you – perhaps a chance for a moment of intimacy between the two of you. Back with the takeaway juice, I find a despondent Leon. Nevertheless, I enjoy the relief on your face as you slowly sip some of the sweet juice.

As I wipe your face with a wet facecloth, I ask: 'What time did you go in?'

'About 1 am.'

They do work around the clock. I even feel sorry for the surgeons who seem to be stretched beyond the reasonable. Could they do a good job under such conditions? How did they feel repairing suicide damage instead of being at home with their families?

'And when did you come round?'

'It took four and a half hours. They had to reopen that one' – your eyes rest on your right hand, the one that had been previously stitched – 'as well as do the big repairs on that one' – your eyes go to your left hand, the most damaged one. It is too early to say if the surgery has been successful.

Tuesday 5 November 2002

Oceane

More nurses this morning, shift after shift. One stood out, a man in his fifties, who just looked and spoke to me like he was deeply sorry that I was in this situation. He had a very soft voice, with an accent, maybe Eastern European. It was the first time I didn't feel judged for my actions, but rather actually seen as a person suffering. The best bit: he connected me to the internet.

Cécile brings in her laptop for me and I read my emails: about uni, about my horse, Freya. The replies from friends that I wrote to before my suicide give me an intense buzz. I feel nearly high from the connections. I also feel ethereally light from having eaten and drunk so little and vomited so much. I sense an almost manic undertone though. I can be ecstatically excited about something and feel the most intense rush of positivity and life force, and then crash down with a complete sense of hopelessness only minutes later.

The possibility that I haven't ruined everything feeds my highs; according to one email I receive from a lecturer, I can go back to uni, finish the year, pretend this never happened. Ben, Alice and Dina visit and it makes me feel even happier and lighter. I can imagine returning to uni with these friends around me. But what's happening here in hospital triggers the lows. The worst parts of the day are the visits from registrars coming to 'chat' to me, asking the same questions over and over. All their negativity; telling me that I will be scheduled for a long time, frowning on me like a naughty child, trying to catch me out with a lie.

This morning with Dr C was the absolute worst. It seems ironic that the only registrar who I have seen a second time since being in hospital is the one I find the most difficult to deal with. Dr C came in, asked the usual questions and I went through the motions, giving her the rundown. What I say is slightly different every time depending on what I've been thinking about that day, or what I think this latest psychiatrist wants to hear. I was particularly over it this morning and I was pretty brief with my answers. Her responses came across as aggressive and sometimes I felt like I couldn't even finish a sentence before she jumped ahead, filling in the information for me. She seemed to have made up her own mind about what had caused me to attempt suicide and she refused to have a bar of anything that I might actually have wanted to say about it.

Then she told me that she had spoken to people at the college and that someone had told her that I was still actively suicidal and would take the first chance I could to end my life. I was furious at her for speaking to people without asking me or at least telling me beforehand. And I feel doubly betrayed by whoever told her that. I am proud of myself that I have not told anyone about my continuing daydreams of suicide. It has taken so much strength NOT to say anything, and now that power has been devalued.

After telling me about her visit to college, she exploded about everything I had not said in my answers. She seemed to have gathered all the pieces of the puzzle, the exact number of pills and all the rest, from previous registrars' notes and she threw it at me like a scorned wife throwing the proof of an affair at her husband.

It was clear to me that she interpreted my omissions as an attempt to deceive her, rather than entertaining the possibility that perhaps I didn't feel the need to repeat myself yet again. I've seen at least one if not two or three different psychiatric registrars every damn day, all with their questions and often a sense of running late for someone else. And yet I am punished for not repeating the exact same detail every time. And it's not like a fun conversation – each time they are asking me about the most distressing memories and traumas of both my whole life and the last few days – and no one seems to give a toss about how it feels to go over it again and again with strangers.

I felt she was proud to have 'found me out', triumphantly waving the evidence at me. She talked about trying to find another bed elsewhere and I feel that my pleas to not be sent to a psych ward will probably just make her try harder to do just that.

What I could not seem to make her understand was that I was not trying to hide anything, or at least not any of the things she was accusing me of hiding.

Cécile

Leon needs a day at home. He has not really landed yet. The many stories brought back from his year of travelling have been force-shelved.

On my way to the City to see you I go to the shops for the little bits you asked me to get you – undies, a phone card, a bottle of your best red grapefruit juice. I also bring my laptop, so you can send and receive emails. Today your watcher is a friendly, dark-haired, middle-aged male nurse. His heavily lined, angular face betrays familiarity with hardship. He actually looks at me and says hello as I come through the door and he stays. He rejoices at the sight of the laptop I pull out of my backpack. You too seem very pleased about it – such signs of pleasure on your drawn face soften my pain and give me hope.

In the hour that follows, we are all joining skills to connect you to the net. At one moment, the nurse finds himself near me and whispers:

'So sad to see that ...'

There is no judgement in his comment, just genuine sadness. It is comforting to see a nurse who shows feelings and treats us like normal humans. With him, you become a person, as he helps you connect with the world out there. When we manage to get you hooked up, your face lights up and we all clap.

Later in the morning we are told that you do not need to be in an orthopaedic unit anymore and that the hospital is trying to find a bed somewhere else for you. You are hoping you can stay in the area so your friends can come and visit you. But there might not be much choice as it is so hard to find a bed anywhere. This is what we have all read in the papers: people waiting everywhere for hospital beds. There is a frustration in the air. I can see what a hard job the nursing staff have.

I am still with you when the psychiatrist arrives.

'Number nine,' you say, rolling your eyes in frustration.

You allow me to stay. We are both hopeful that some positive solution will be found.

The psychiatrist is a young woman, in her late twenties, tall, with long dark hair, who sits close to you on one side of the bed while I sit on the other. She seems friendly. When the question of finding a bed comes up and you ask if you could stay in the area, she becomes cold and angry, staring at me off and on as if she is making sure that I listen to what she has to say:

'You did not tell me in my first visit that not only had you slashed your wrists and taken over a hundred tablets, but that you also tried to suffocate yourself with a plastic bag, and to hang yourself with the belt of your nightgown. You didn't tell me! Because of that, you will have to be hospitalised in a high-security psych unit.'

She sounds like a judge reading out her guilty verdict in a criminal court, because you have 'lied'. Does she think it is that simple? Is this what you've been subjected to by psychiatrists one to eight? Do any of them remember their pledge to do no harm?

And does this psychiatrist realise it is the first time I am hearing all this?

What is she hoping for from showing such anger? To shock me? To frighten me? To provoke you? Has she decided that you are just trying to fool everybody? Can't she see that you need gentleness, understanding?

She leaves and we look at each other, totally dismayed.

I think of my suicidal clients who would rather kill themselves than be hospitalised again. I don't think I will ever again be able to tell these clients that the hospital will give them a safe place to rest and be looked after.

Later on, a nurse comes to announce that there is a bed for you at another hospital, which she says will probably work out very well as it is closer to my home in the Mountains. Well actually, no, it does not work out very well, because I will travel wherever you are, but once there you won't get visits from your friends. Especially as they are all starting their exams. They are sending you into exile. You are so upset and disappointed.

I am desperate to help: 'Oceane, I am going to tell your psychiatrist that it is not a possibility because of a boundary issue to do with my work. I could have clients there and it wouldn't be appropriate if I came across them.'

'Please,' you beg, 'I do not want to be sent so far away from all my friends.'

I rush to the front desk and explain to the nurse that I need to talk to your psychiatrist urgently. They reach her on the phone. I explain briefly. She dismisses my argument. I insist. In the end she gives in: she agrees to talk to her supervisor. Half an hour of rushed phone calls between nurse, psychiatrist, head psychiatrist, all trying to change the course of things. I beg for you to be put in a general ward, or be kept on this one, till another bed is freed in this area.

The head nurse comes:

'We can't provide a twenty-four-hour watch here any longer. We are terribly understaffed. I cannot stretch my nurses any more.'

I promise her I will stay by you; I will be your nurse, your watcher; I will sleep on the chair next to your bed. The head nurse of the orthopaedic ward is on the verge of tears, torn between her sympathy and her professional constraints. None of this is her fault. She too is caught up in a system that seems to be killing you rather than helping you want to live.

In the end, I am not allowed to be your watcher. They cannot take the risk, given you are scheduled.

A call comes in for the head nurse. As she puts the handset down, she turns to me:

'The ambulance is here. I am sorry but there is nothing else we can do. Oceane has to go.'

Oceane

Dr C came back a few hours after her morning rant at me and told me I have to move to another hospital. I am so scared of what this means – both because it is so far away, and because it is a psychiatric unit. This morning, having a few emails, a visit from Ben and Dina and the interaction with the kind nurse was the first ray of optimism I've had. The forced move makes it feel like I will go back down the drain. I had in my mind that if I said it wasn't the right thing for me, and if I could explain why I couldn't cope, they would listen. The feeling of disempowerment when Dr C said, 'Tough: you have to go,' was awful. I could feel myself physically sinking. She's probably delighted to dole out this punishment.

At least I feel Cécile is on my side. She tried so hard to argue with them. I could sense her desperation to make them find another solution. I think she knows that this might tip me over the edge, and she is not wrong.

Within an hour of Dr C's bad news, a nurse comes

and tells me the ambulance is here to transport me. It was apparently a done deal before they even told me.

I didn't say it to you, Mama, but thank you for fighting for me.

Cécile

I feel I have failed. I return to your room, resigned.

'I am sorry, Oceane. I'm going to follow the ambulance.'

I do not want you to be left alone.

You ask me if I can first drive to your college and pick up some stuff that friends of yours were going to bring to you at hospital. It's all been arranged: they'll be waiting for me in the car park.

The college car park is familiar from dropping you off or collecting things for you. I remember the Sunday night just a week before your suicide attempt. We had a lovely weekend together in the Mountains – you'd been coming up regularly for a few months, supposedly to prepare Freya. You were going to lease her; the cost of keeping her in the City had become prohibitive and you could not give her the attention and work-out she needed. You were selling your car too. You had bought it to get to Freya, it had got broken into at college and you needed the money for your planned summer travels in Europe. So, in my blind mind, it made sense. How did I not read all these signs?

These weekends were the most balanced, gentle, flowing we had ever had. Just the two of us. I never realised they were your goodbye weekends. Were they actually? Did the excitement and lightness come once the decision to suicide was made, or did you still have some hope to live?

While we were driving back and forth between the City and the Mountains, you asked me a lot of questions about our family. I talked to you about the early days of our family, and how I saw some of its problems. You seemed to lap it up. I told you old family stories. Did that push you more into despair, or did it help at all? So many of the family stories have a dark undertone. Will you ever tell me? You seemed happy. 'I really enjoyed learning about your life,' you wrote in an email, in which you seemed to be longing for peace and calm. I never thought that you could only see death to bring you that peace.

You seemed pressed for time to complete a couple of assignments. I thought how good it was to see you for once doing an assignment at the last minute. You usually always started on them so early. You were becoming a normal student – last-minute rush. They all do that. Now I learn that you were late because you did not intend to be there to give them in. Oceane, I did not get it.

I did not get it when you frantically sorted out your old clothes. There was an excitement in your urgency. I thought: 'Waow! She is getting rid of the clutter before going overseas – getting rid of the old before entering the new.' You insisted we had to get the bags to the op shop – except for two thick, warm and comfortable jumpers you were determined to give me.

I did not get it, Oceanette, I did not get it.

That last Sunday night you offered to go back to the City by train, but you were so tired that I insisted I drive you back to college. When we arrived at the car park, you gave me a big hug: 'Thank you so much for driving me all the way.' I did not get it.

As I pull up in that same car park this afternoon, a cluster of strangers is waiting for me with a box and a bag of things. One older man introduces himself as the dean of the college and shakes my hand. Not too many words are exchanged. What to say? I am too exhausted and worried about where you are being moved.

'Give our love to Oceane!'

And carrying this cheerful greeting to you, I drive off across the City to find you, trying to keep calm and stay focused for my own safety.

Notes from hospital division of mental health

Reason for Admission

Transferred to us after 5 day stay in ICU and recovery from surgical repair of tendons following serious suicide attempt by cutting, attempted hanging, and overdose in context of major depression following a sexual assault.

Progress in Hospital

Unhappy at being hospitalised in a psychiatric unit. When in ICU, required 'special' nurse because of concern at suicidal ideation. However, on transfer, she appeared calm, euthymic and reactive. There was some concern that she might be hiding ongoing suicidal thoughts because of ongoing stress stemming from sexual assault. However she guaranteed her safety.

Referral Letter

Dear Dr P.

Thank you for accepting Oceane, an 18yo woman who was transferred to us from ICU following a high lethality suicide attempt. She cut both forearms lacerating flexor tendons, median nerve then took 3 temazepam, woke up and overdosed on 90 paracetamol, then put a bag over her head and then tried to strangle herself. She called a friend who took her to emergency at the local hospital. This is in the context of stressors involving [...] a sexual assault that occurred at uni early this year and a family history of early childhood abuse. Oceane describes 2/12 hx [two-month history] of depressed mood which she states is not pervasive with neurovegetative features of decreased concentration and disturbed sleep with initial middle insomnia. Oceane presents as very incongruent in affect, minimalises her attempt and has limited insight into the situation. She does not want to start antidepressants until reviewed by an inpatient psychiatrist. She was on sertraline [Zoloft] 50mg prior to her suicide attempt for about 1 week and she found it extremely agitating, she attributes her attempt to the sertraline. She is not on psychotropic medication at present. There is a strong family history of depression on the mother's side with three of Oceane's aunts suffering from depression. Oceane denies ongoing suicidal ideation but collateral info from the dean of her college states a few students have reported that Oceane is expressing ongoing suicidal ideation to friends and that she is regretful that she did not succeed. There is grave concern for her from us, the community mental health centre and university. She is not allowed to return to the boarding house.

Oceane

This place is unbearable. Physically and emotionally. I feel it on every level of my being.

The ambulance trip ended up being uplifting, despite my mood and the oddity of travelling flat on my back.

The bubbly Irish lady who rode with me distracted me so well. I could see her reading over my chart for a few minutes. Then she looked up at me and said, 'Now, what made you go and do that to yourself?' Funny how she could ask the same question as the nurse the other day, but instead of making me shut down, it felt refreshing.

I guess suicide must be a very strange concept for someone who isn't suicidal.

She chatted with me openly and I could make some dry jokes about the situation, which felt good. The psychiatrists don't seem to accept humour about this – which I can understand, but after answering 'how do you feel now?', 'do you still feel suicidal?', 'are you wishing it had been successful?' a million times, it is nice to be able to laugh and be asked fresh questions.

I could feel my anxiety rise as we arrived at this hospital an hour or so later. It helped that Cécile was here.

The first thing I noticed as I was being admitted into the psych ward was an old lady shuffling along the corridor – she was the stereotypical 'crazy lady'. There were people muttering, women with beards hunched over, sounds of tortured people: groaning, moaning, guttural sounds. I wanted to tell someone, 'Wow, this really is just like *One Flew Over the Cuckoo's Nest*!' I guess I could have told you, Cécile, but I am used to keeping thoughts in my head.

My overriding thought was I NEED TO GET OUT OF HERE. I could feel the urge to die rushing through me, and not disappearing. For the first time since being in hospital I stopped caring about the pain; I just knew I had to kill myself rather than stay here.

Cécile and I filled out the paperwork together. We were sat on a tiny narrow bed in a room that looked like a school camp: narrow beds, one after the other, and tiny generic bedside tables. The form had a depression scale to fill out, which felt a little ironic. What should I say to 'how many times in the last week have you felt life was not worth living'? How did they want me to measure that? There wasn't room on the form to say 'actually, I was starting to regain my will to live three hours ago, but since arriving here, all I want to do is top myself as quickly as possible'.

Thank God I had Cécile there. I didn't tell her, but I hope she knew that it was making the situation more bearable.

After the form filling, we sat out in the cafeteria section. Everywhere here feels like being in a zoo, with a sense that you are being watched from all sides, at all times. 'All the better to see you with,' I could picture the wolf saying to Little Red Riding Hood.

We sat at a picnic-style table. They'd given us little packets of Jatz crackers and cheap, nasty cheese – useless to me because I have big open sores down my throat from being intubated for so long. Eating mush is painful enough; I can't even imagine managing a cracker.

A boy – or man maybe – came up and tried engaging with us. He looked scary, with an intense stare. I wanted to scream at someone, 'HAVE YOU NOT BEEN LISTENING? I am traumatised and vulnerable because of an assault that triggered a downhill spiral which finished with me slitting my wrists and swallowing as many pills as I could. Why are you putting me in a situation where I feel threatened by this man?'

Luckily Cécile sensed my terror, and we removed ourselves from the cafeteria. But I need to remove myself from this place. I don't feel safe. I want to tell them that there has been a mistake; I shouldn't be here, I am not crazy like these other people. Who knows, maybe they weren't crazy either when they first arrived – a few nights here would tip anyone over the edge, I think. I sense that these nurses do not give a fuck about the patients; that if I make too much fuss, they'll just send me to the ECT room or jab me with a sedative like in the movies. How could I ever get better in a place that I feel absolutely terrified in?

We waited forever for the psychiatrist. I didn't understand at first what we were waiting for. It seems that being scheduled means I am not a person, and therefore don't need to be told what is happening.

Finally, at about midnight, the psychiatrist arrived. We sat in a huge room with couches and toys – like a family therapy room. She had that slightly harried look of an overworked person – wild hair sticking out a bit – but seemed very friendly and willing to engage, and I was comforted that she was an older lady. All the psychs I had seen so far had been young, and had a hardness about them, like they were still following their lecture notes or the rulebook they were given on their first day.

This psychiatrist went through the usual questions. Yes, I still have two older brothers. Yes, I still have separated parents, just like the last thousand times I've been asked.

I tried to tell her that I had told this story so many times this week. I wanted her to know that I wasn't being blasé; it's just that I keep opening my heart to these psychiatrists, and they take a few notes and then walk out and I don't see them again. And then another one walks in, and on it goes.

Another thing I find hard about these consults is that each psych seems to decide what they think is 'worthy' or justifies a suicide attempt and hone in on that: jump on it and shake it up like a dog with a bone. This psych seems to have chosen the family history and dynamics. By the time I realise this is where she is headed, I can't seem to redirect the focus to what is more important to me: all the things from the last six months with Seth and the college. Maybe I was damaged before, but what happened earlier in the year broke me. I didn't have the energy to explain – I'd been crying so much in the last hour that I had a huge headache.

It was strange doing the consult with Cécile – especially talking about the family stuff. I wonder what it sounds like to her. It must be awful to hear these stories laid bare by your suicidal daughter.

When the psych told me that I don't have a choice about being here, it was another kick in the guts after a long day of being kicked. They've told me I have to take sleeping pills, which I tried to refuse, but like everything else here, I have no choice. I think about slipping the pills out of my mouth to save them up for an overdose, but they are standing over me as I take them and I am terrified of the consequences if they caught me.

Clinical notes from registrar

Personal Hx: Lived with family up until graduated Y10. Y11 & Y12 – Moved out of home. Very bright student, HSC 97%. At present psychology student at university.

Young Caucasian girl with plasters on both forearms. Good eye contact. Cooperative. Speech at Normal rate and volume. Mood is euthymic, affect is congruent, reactive.

TF Normal.

TC Denied suicidal ideation.

Denied psychotic symptoms. Oriented in Time, Place and Person.

Cécile

At the hospital I pull into the visitors' car park, very desolate in the dark, and find my way to admissions. The foyer is poorly lit; the hospital has settled for the night.

The woman behind the desk seems resentful at being interrupted reading her magazine and is not very generous in giving directions, leaving me to wander through a maze of shabby, eerily deserted, half-lit corridors, and staircases that seem to lead to more corridors, with a few mostly unhelpful signs and doors made of thick, aged and scratched plastic.

Eventually – I am not sure how – I do find my way to the psych unit.

I have forgotten that 'high security' means double doors and bells and somebody coming to let you in.

I am shown to the front desk and find you there, still in your wheelchair. You look lost, silently terrified. A nurse is just putting away the few personal belongings you have with you: mobile phone, keys, Discman, all deemed dangerous. Stripped bare. Like a criminal.

'Could I have a drink?' you ask shyly.

The nurse goes into a central nurses' station, an insulated square room, all windows from halfway up, and comes back with a glass of water which she pushes towards you. I intercept the glass. *She cannot use her hands. Can't you see?*

'Would you have a straw so she *can* drink?'

The nurse looks angry. I am sure she would prefer to chat away with her colleagues in what I have named 'the fish tank'. I imagine they curse late arrivals that interrupt their crosswords or card games.

'Come with me, I'll show you your bed.'

We follow the nurse to a ward. There, she points to the last free bed: a narrow, bare bunk. We are in a jail. Three other patients are snoring and mumbling.

'That's your bed. The psychiatrist has been paged and will be here to see you in an hour or so.'

This must be so horrifying for you. At least I have seen psych wards before, in France, on the occasions I visited my little sister. It's funny how similar they seem to be from one end of the world to another. I've heard the raving and shuffling, seen the haggard looks and the slowed-down gait of the over-sedated. You haven't.

This place is not for you. You are neither mad nor drugged-up silly. You are just very fragile. Only a week ago you were trying very hard to kill yourself and you are just out after hours of surgery, after days of waiting with no food and hardly any fluid in your body. You are on the edge of a cliff wondering whether life is liveable. How can they, how dare they treat you like this? They are probably more concerned with ticking the boxes so as to cover their arses than actually helping you. I have heard these stories from my clients. I have seen one sister turned into a vegetable with overmedication and diabetic coma treatment. I have seen my eldest sister after electroshocks. Not you, my child. No!

We sit next to each other on the bunk, our backs resting against the wall, knees up to our chests. We both feel frightened, helpless and exhausted. Images of deportation and refugees, miserable and terrified, huddled in railway stations, on pavements, in camp dormitories, flash through my mind. It is a balmy summer night and I am shivering.

The nurse brings a form. 'You need to fill this out.'

She cannot even write, can't you see?

'Your rights are stated on a sheet of paper you will find in the drawer of the side table. It would be a good idea to read it after you have filled out the form.'

We keep ourselves busy and awake filling the form, you telling me what to write. When it's time to sign, you struggle to hold the pen and shape some oversized, hardly readable letters.

I reach for the rights sheet. It looks like the regulations you find in caravans and motel rooms. Only this is to remind you that you are scheduled, that you have lost your right to make decisions, followed by the dry language of legal procedures for appeals and reviews in case you do not agree with the treatment imposed. In writing, it is all so human and respectful. And a 'not sane of mind' person is supposed to understand this legal jargon? I am almost surprised not to find a Bible in the drawer. Second commandment: Thou shall not attempt to take thy own life.

The exhaustion takes over and, leaning on each other's shoulder, we doze off.

'Look at them!' A warm voice wakes us, seemingly touched by our closeness.

I open one eye.

'I am Dr So-and-so. You are Oceane?'

'Yes,' you say, trying to wake up.

'Sorry to be so late, I had an emergency. Let's find a place to talk.'

I look at my watch – 11.30 pm. We follow the woman: my sort of age, vivacious, a bit plump, short wavy hair and thick glasses. 'Number ten,' you tell me, rolling your eyes.

We follow her to the front desk, where she asks if she can have the key to the family therapy room. The nurse walks us there and unlocks the door to a room left untidy at the end of the day: armchairs turned all directions, cheap plastic toys lying around, a messy pile of old magazines on a low table, pillows disarranged on a sofa. We all sit. The psychiatrist looks straight into your eyes.

'So, Oceane, tell me what's happened?'

Hope is there, once again. Hope for what? I am not sure; probably hope for your release. Maybe hope for understanding, help and good treatment.

After a long interview the psychiatrist takes a large breath and looks you even more straight in the eyes:

'All the statistics say that people who try to suicide once do it again. So we have to keep you in this unit; you realise you are scheduled, don't you?'

You have been trying to hold yourself together to speak and now I see you being broken once more. You sob:

'I can't stay here, please, can I be in a normal ward for the night? My mum will stay with me.'

'No, you have to be on twenty-four-hour watch and

your mum is not allowed to stay with you during the night anyway.'

On these words, and with no further explanation, she gets up and leaves us there, stunned. We have no idea as to what is happening. I help you to the sofa. You are a sobbing mess.

Does Number Ten think that this is going to help you stay alive? Do these psychiatrists even realise they keep breaking you? I can't imagine them taking any responsibility if you end up snapping and killing yourself. To them you will just be a statistic, not even one to learn from.

You plead: 'Please, please, can you do something?'

I feel so powerless myself, caught in this prison-like machinery. Number Ten has just left us locked in this windowless room somewhere in a maze of corridors, away from any other human presence. I cannot bear the idea of having to leave you here.

I try to calm you, wiping the mucus and tears that are covering your face and stroking your long wet hair away from the mess. There is not even water to cool your burning eyes. It is the middle of the night and I realise that by now, nothing much can be achieved. We wait on the sofa, in our mess of tears, tissues and caresses.

Eventually a woman comes in, young, tall and thin, with long, loose blondish hair and a friendly smile which until now I would have trusted. The admissions nurse who took away your belongings and showed you your bed is following her. She is almost in tears herself. Maybe she is human after all, caught too between doing her job and feeling for you.

The new woman does not mention who she is, or why the psychiatrist left. She explains once more that you are scheduled and what it means: no, they won't put you in a normal ward even if I sit with you all night. There is no point fighting. They are definitely more concerned about covering themselves in case you kill yourself and I sue them.

I launch into a last desperate attempt to negotiate the possibly negotiable – maybe the difference between still having a daughter by tomorrow morning or being called to view a corpse and having to listen to people say they are very sorry.

'Please, could you at least find a medical bed for Oceane? She can't use her hands; she won't be safe in a narrow bed on the ward and with one pillow only. Can you see? She still needs propping; she needs the width and raised side of a medical bed.' And also, I dare: 'Please could you find a quieter room? The patients in her room were carrying on as if no one was there. Oceane has been through a lot. She needs a bit more quiet.'

The young woman's face stiffens for a flicker of a second, but she seems to have seen that I am not trying to be difficult. A beam of humanity crosses her eyes.

'I'll see what I can do' – and she walks to the door, once again leaving us not knowing much, but with a little twig of hope to hang on to. She returns after twenty minutes.

'I have found a medical bed and we've found a room with just one other patient.'

'Oh, thank you so much,' I say.

You are beyond responding.

The young woman leads us to the room where your bed has already been wheeled.

'That's all I can do.'

'Thank you, that is much better.'

'And she can have her Discman,' she tells the night nurse as she leaves: a bit of unexpected warmth, permission, being treated as a normal teenager.

There is a glimpse of comfort as I help you undress and settle into a more familiar, less jail-like bed and the nurse brings in your Discman. But then, as I am sitting on the edge of the bed while you get your awkward packs of plaster and iodised fingers to organise a bit of music, I feel scared again. What if they have pushed you over and you use the thin electric cord to try to kill yourself? They cannot see that locking you up does not make you safe. It just puts you at risk of doing something stupid to get out of the nightmare. Do they really believe one cannot kill oneself in their 'high security ward'?

A nurse I haven't seen before arrives with sleeping pills.

'I don't really want them; I'll be all right,' you tell him.

'Everybody takes them here,' he says curtly. 'Don't think you are different.'

Once again, I am shocked at the aggression, but I do not intervene; I am too exhausted and any remark would probably attract more aggression. If only you knew, I instead say to myself. This is nothing about being different: since she swallowed the hundred or so tablets, she has refused all medication except what has been forced into her veins through needles. Maybe it is a good sign. I don't even know myself. But I can tell you she is not trying to be difficult or different. She is only trying to survive or not to survive, and I'll do all I can to help her choose to survive.

I leave, promising you I'll be there first thing in the morning.

Back home, after a couple of hours' sleep, I wake up in a startle, haunted again by the dread that you might try to use the Discman cord. I call. The night nurse promises they are keeping an eye on you. I have no choice but to try to trust her.

Wednesday 6 November 2002

Oceane

The positive of the sleeping pills is that I slept the sleep of the dead. It is like an anaesthetic: you cannot tell the moment it knocks you out, and then six hours later it catapults you back into the woken world without any warning.

I feel strangely empty and hollow, after all the crying and emotion of yesterday and the exhaustion of the late night and the intensity of my fear about being here. It is still the worst nightmare I could imagine, but there is something a little bit easier this morning. I think it is because of the depth of my sleep, and the light of day rather than the midnight madness of last night.

Cécile

I turn up at the door of the psych unit at 6.30 am sharp. Yes, says the nurse, you are awake. Yes, I can go in. You are sitting up in your bed propped up with tidy pillows, the Discman next to you, cord and all.

You greet me with a smile.

'Did you manage to sleep?'

Yes, you did. You look more rested than last night, yet still worried. What is today going to bring?

'Would you like me to do your hair?'

I brush and plait your hair. It has lost its shine from the lack of washing and fresh air, and probably the drugs still running through your blood.

We tidy up the few things lying around your bed and bedside table – enjoying the little bit of what feels like some control and order over your life and readying ourselves. For what? We don't know.

A nurse comes in. She explains that the registrar should be here to see you sometime this morning, but cannot say exactly when. She looks at me:

'You can help her with her shower if you want.'

'Yes, sure,' I reply automatically, realising immediately that I have no idea how to do it.

'I'll give you waterproof stuff to put over her casts.'

We gather a few clean clothes and walk to the fish tank. The nurse presents me with a neat pile of towels, a bar of soap, shampoo and plastic mittens with overlong arms.

'You just stick these on and tape them over and you'll be fine. Put a lot of tape all over – the casts must not get wet.'

She walks us to a spacious shower with plenty of room for two people to move around. That's good, we'll be able to keep our clothes dry.

'You can lock the door if you want.'

Another little sign of trust. We lock the door and stand there awkwardly.

I become matter-of-fact.

'Let's have a look at this stuff. Hang on. First I'll put the towel and clean clothes on this door hook. They should stay dry there. Maybe you should take your clothes off first, before we get these plastic things on.'

You strip, simply, quietly, and I try to hide my surprise at your woman's body. You haven't let me see your body naked for many years. Showering you is attached to memories of your child's body. We both do what needs to be done, silently negotiating the line between this forced intimacy and respect for your powerlessness.

'I'll just try and get the water right before you get in.'

I lean into the shower, directing the head away from me and play around with the temperature of the water. I would hate you being shocked by too hot or too cold water. Luckily, the temperature and water flow remain even.

You step in cautiously. Yes, it is good. While you stand under the water, I undress to my undies so I can soap you.

After I have washed your hair, you ask if I can rub your back. I notice scars on your thighs, but say nothing. More that I do not know. What else will I discover? Then I go and sit on the plastic chair in the corner while you enjoy the water running over your body and face – a time of your own.

'That was good! I feel better.'

'I bet you do! So good we could wash your hair!'

Delicately, we pull the plastic mittens off. Get some clothes on you. Every gesture is slow and cautious so you do not wet your casts or fall. You look less like a patient with your jeans on and the top we found that can slip on over the casts.

'They are still in there!' I hear a nurse in the distance. Yes, it takes time. I finish dressing myself and we open the door. It's been a lot and you look exhausted and ready to go and lie on your bed – but first we have to pass the mutterings, shuffling feet and strange looks on the way.

Oceane

After my awkward but oh-so-enjoyed shower, yet another psychiatrist arrives to assess me. I am relieved when I see it is a different doctor to last night. I feel an enormous amount of pressure to get it right this time. To get myself out of this hospital. I am confident that my survival is dependent on me getting out of here.

With the succession of psychiatrists who have assessed me, I have tried to play the game in the way that I think will help me the most. Telling them parts of the story over others, downplaying the number of ways in which I attempted to kill myself, focusing on the impact of the Zoloft and how extreme the side effects were. I thought I was being smart, but now feel like some of it has backfired, making them think that I am changing my story or that I have little insight into the situation.

So when Dr Martin comes in and introduces himself, I put every bit of me into the conversation. I am the most clear-headed I've been for a long time. Life, everything, is riding on this.

'I've had a tough year,' I begin.

Dr Martin smiles back at me. And finally I can breathe out a little.

Dr Martin is more open, friendlier – there is something different in how he listens to me. He doesn't try to lead the conversation.

I talk through the assault at the start of the year, the spiralling down, the self-hatred, the constant re-traumatising reminder of having 'him' present in my living space, intimidating me. I talk about my childhood and how my sense of vulnerability was exacerbated by the feeling of not being safe in my own family. Then I tell him about trying to get help but having one counsellor talk to me about finding God and another one who was just not able to cope with the situation, and told me so. I talk about resisting Zoloft, and how it disempowered me further. I tell Dr Martin that I can't tolerate this environment and that I just want to be home and to start rebuilding my life. I tell him how it gave me a glimmer of hope to hear from my course coordinator that I could still finish my year, that other students were even taking notes for me.

I get to the end feeling unburdened and hopeful, but also apprehensive that this will end like all the other psych consults.

Giving nothing away, he leaves and speaks to Cécile while I sit on my bed and try not to get myself into a panic about the situation. I just have to try not to think about what it would mean if I am stuck here longer. I resist the urge to dream of my suicide method if I am told I have to stay. I feel less safe in the hospital than I did alone and lost in my college room a week earlier.

Cécile

Forty-five minutes later, the registrar calls me.

'Can we have a chat?'

He takes me to an empty room and asks me about you and the family.

We've had a difficult family, but you have always been the easy and quiet one.

'She said your relationship had not been good in the past but that in the last year it has improved.'

'Yes, we've been able to talk more.'

'Would you look after her?'

'Of course I will look after her. I am concerned because I do not even know exactly what has led her to this.'

'Did she tell you about it?'

'No, she hasn't.'

'There was something with a boy.' He rushes the words.

He obviously does not want to break your confidentiality – or perhaps he does not want to upset me.

Dr Martin tells me he does not think you have to stay in this unit, as long as I am prepared to look after you and organise some therapy.

'Oceane says you are a therapist yourself, so I am sure you can help her find somebody.'

'Of course.'

I sure can, but I don't tell him it won't be a therapist that is a pawn in this system, which, by now, I am certain is broken. I have become so cynical. At least I have a glimmer of hope – I am so relieved at the prospect of 'proper' therapy for you.

He and I walk together to your room. As we come in, you look at him expectantly.

Oceane

Finally, Dr Martin comes back and says, 'Well, you can go home if you want to.'

It is like being told by a parole officer that my sentence has been reduced from life to nothing. I barely know what to say through my wide eyes and huge smile but do manage to tell him that I will call him in a year and tell him that he made the right decision. He laughs, and says, 'I'll wait to hear from you.'

Cécile helps me pack my one or two possessions. We hustle like excited ducks down the corridor, clutching our paperwork from Dr Martin – out past the nurses' station and suddenly into the brightest sunshine.

Other than being wheeled from hospital to ambulance in loading bays, I haven't been outside for an entire week. The air feels so pure, and the sky so bright, and even the light bouncing off the tar and the other cars looks particularly beautiful. I am too scared to even look over my shoulder as we scurry out, terrified that I will see a nurse or psychiatrist running after us to say, 'Sorry, there has been a mistake, Dr Martin doesn't have the authority to release you.' We can't get in the car fast enough and I feel every bit of my body pulsating with adrenalin. It is like a grand escape.

I am so overwhelmed with my freedom and how quickly I've gone from being in the most helpless and hopeless situation to the ecstatic sensation of release. I can see the relief in Cécile too – she must have been holding the same fear as me.

Cécile

As soon as Dr Martin is gone, we pack up. This feels so good after walking out of these hospitals alone, tired, sad, driving home only to rest till I can drive back the following day. Leaving the room behind, bumping into Number Ten, who does not even say hello to us, asking the nurse to get your belongings from the fish tank, being let out through the security doors – this is what walking out of jail must feel like. The light feels too bright.

'I knew what to say and what not to say to be let out,' you say cheekily.

'Is that what happened?'

But then you become more serious. 'He is the first one who took time to listen to me.'

Oceane

Like Thelma and Louise, but a little paler, skinnier and more worn out, we drive across the City to college. I want to see my friends to celebrate.

I can feel the adrenalin slowly winding back; I can feel the previously overwhelming thoughts slowly recede to a normal rate of internal chatter. But then at uni I find Alice, Ben, Dina and I am overly optimistic, bubbly, probably bordering on manic. It's so good to see them back on home turf rather than from the unpleasant angle of a hospital bed with tubes and beeping machines and the exposure of a thin, white hospital gown that is never done up at the back.

I am not sure why I rang Ben from hospital on the Friday, just three days after the attempt. I think it was because I was so lonely and in desperate need of contact with familiar faces. He came straight away with Dina and Alice to see me. I can't imagine what it was like for them – the awkwardness of not knowing what to do or say – but for me it was such a human experience in the depths of the mechanical hospital environment with only strange faces around.

I feel closer to them since my suicide attempt. Like the forced honesty of the situation has broken down a barrier. I only met them nine months ago, and we had had an easy, bantering friendship starting – but I always felt like I couldn't easily participate in conversations. I think where I was in my head and life was too serious for such new friendships, so I mostly kept my mouth shut. I could never think of the right thing to say, or by the time I felt like I could slip into a gap in the conversation, it had moved on to another topic.

But all of a sudden, since being in hospital, the friendship is like an old trusted one.

Cécile

Arriving home later that night, the house looks beautiful, softly lit and tidy. Leon has cleaned up and prepared a dinner. We both help you to the sofa, fussing to make you comfortable. You are so happy to be home. I am going to sleep well tonight.

Thursday 7 November 2002

Oceane

I wake with the utter calmness and relief of being freed from hospital, and the luxury of a double bed and a doona and soft pillows.

I can hear Cécile up and about, and the deeply familiar noises of the house: creaking floorboards, the sound the hot water system makes when fired up, the raucous cries of birds and other animals outside, and the crackling of the tin roof adjusting as the sun warms it up.

I feel more at home here than I have for a long time. I can feel the pleasure of happy memories bubbling up inside me for the first time in ages.

I turn to one side and see the little square of wall that I framed years ago, where the different layers of paint can all be seen. The layer of pink of the original house, the blue that Leon chose when it was his room, the yellow that I chose when it became my room. It symbolises not only the change that this room has undergone but the autonomy and trust we had as kids – painting was just one of those little joyful things we got to do when we swapped bedrooms.

When I call out 'Mama!' Cécile comes in and it is so peaceful to slowly wake up with her sitting on the bed, chatting through details, logistics and plans. I feel a bit like a baby bird, all fragile and vulnerable and weak. Light as a feather in my body and my mind. Even though I have been dreaming of this moment and wishing for it more than anything else, all of a sudden I don't know what to do with myself. I haven't dared think beyond my ambition to leave hospital. But now what? What does 'being home' mean? Will I be OK? How will this work?

I start with a bath. I can feel every bit of my skin tingle; it feels so alive after having had contact with only a hospital gown or hospital sheets.

As we put the plastic bags over my casts and secure them with tape, I have a flashback of putting the plastic bag over my head after I'd taken my pills and using sticky tape to secure it tightly around my neck with no accidental gaps for oxygen. I keep thinking to myself: 'Why didn't that work?' I have to push the thoughts out of my head because it makes me feel wobbly to remember the details of those twenty-four hours. I desperately want to enjoy this moment – this sweet and light feeling of being safe and nurtured.

I feel nearly in shock with my new-found freedom and my cleanliness post-bath. I can't decide what I want to do first. Call friends? Go to the shops? Even studying appeals – I think to the part of me that wants to prove that I am planning for the future, that I am OK, that it was the right decision to let me out of hospital.

Late in the afternoon we go to Dr Loxton. This is one of the 'tick boxes' I have committed to as a condition of being out of hospital. I haven't seen him in years. I have a good memory of him as my GP, but I feel quite apprehensive. My secret fear, of course, is that I will be sent back to hospital.

He is happy to see me again after so long, and it makes me very shy about telling him why I have two arms in plaster. I realise suddenly that this is my first experience of telling someone who doesn't know what has happened.

At least he is a genuine listener; I can sense his surprise at the efforts I went to in my attempt – and again I am secretly pleased about that. I am being taken seriously. Dr Loxton doesn't think that I was just trying to get attention or that it was a cry for help. And it helps combat the embarrassment at having failed at something. Even if that thing was taking my life.

We go over our allotted fifteen minutes, but Dr Loxton doesn't seem to mind and is very still and present in his attention. Again, like the older nurse, there is something comforting about having a mature, parent-like figure looking after me right now. Whatever the cause, it is a positive moment of connection to put in my bank – I need to rebuild those reserves.

Cécile is in the waiting room and I feel genuinely happy when I see her. I am very mindful of how good it feels to be walking out of a medical environment voluntarily.

The hardest conversation today is the negotiations with Cécile around my care. It is a running conversation that started this morning when she came and sat on the bed with me and has continued all day. We've entered and left the conversation – interrupted by the bathing, shopping and chores. Now we are back into it. Am I allowed to sleep in my room on my own? Yes – no negotiation there. Do I mind if there is an intercom? I guess it's fine if it means Cécile would be happier. Would the intercom have to be on all night? Surely not. How many minutes can I be alone during the day?

We negotiate, brainstorm and then negotiate some more. It is a reminder of what I have done and what the future holds. I still have a fantasy that everything can just go back to normal. That I can pretend this never happened until either I've found my will to live again or till I've regained my strength to finish the job I started. I don't like this middle ground – having to face the consequences of my actions and being trapped by them. Being watched, negotiating the rules. I'm not used to this. I've been so independent for so many years, even before I moved out of home really.

Cécile

I wake up early, feeling guilty for having slept all night. The house is unusually quiet. I go and check that you are all right. As I get close I hear your voice, 'Mama!' and pop my head through the door of your bedroom. Still smiling, still relieved to be at home.

You have slept off and on. With both arms in casts propped up with lots of pillows, you could not move and had to lie awake for long stretches of time. After helping you drink, I lie next to you. A time to talk while the phone is quiet and the air is still cool. A small island of togetherness.

'I am not depressed anymore!' you announce.

I am so glad to have you here, Oceanette. I just want to nurse you back into life.

Our first day is like the first day after a baby is born. Your first bath – making sure the bathtub is really clean, the temperature is just right, making sure you do not slip. Holding, supporting and sponging gently. These scars on your thighs again ... Do I say something? Do I pretend I haven't seen them?

You look like a queen now that you have been dried and dressed, and propped up with pillows on the lounge, mobile and cordless phones easily reachable. Today the shopping list is unusual: straws for drinking, nourishing yet light foods that your liver will tolerate and that will build you up, walkie-talkie so you can call me at night, long waterproof mittens, shower head you can use in the bath.

The phone rings. A family friend: 'How is our girl doing?'

'She is home; I was allowed to take her home.' We all rejoice.

Community mental health calls. 'Could I talk to Oceane?'

'Yes, sure.' They ask you how things are. Of course you say all is fine.

'Won't they come and see you?' I enquire.

'They did not say, they just said they'd call again tomorrow to see how things are.'

In the afternoon we go for our first outing into town. We have overcome your anxiety over the small-town problem of running into familiar faces with a cover story about a horse-riding accident to explain your two casts. You get excited when you come across a colourful hessian shoulder bag – no zip, that's perfect – and a shawl to help hide your arms and take away the problem of sleeves every time the temperature goes up or down.

You enjoy finding things you really like, without worrying about cost. When you were born, we had to rely on food coupons from Vinnies and, with winter coming, we would not be able to keep our home warm. You were too young to remember the times of surviving on pipis and coconuts collected on the beach, and potato seconds at five cents a kilo. Op shops are still our dress shops and money often a worry.

We make our way to your local GP who luckily has time to see you. You want to see him alone. When he walks you back to the reception area, he has tears in his eyes.

Friday 8 November 2002

Oceane

Thirty-six hours out of hospital and we have a routine. When I hear Mama stirring in the kitchen and the familiar sounds of the house waking up, I call out to her and she comes in to touch base. It is a nice time of day – sleepy, safe, private. Then all of a sudden the day is off and running and it seems we are just trying to keep up with it.

Study is the theme today: getting myself set up for a few weeks of prepping for exams. It is an incredibly fine line between motivating myself to study and not getting into a panic where I feel like suiciding just to avoid the pressure of exams. The reality is that doing well at uni (or anywhere else) is important to me – and while it is certainly not the driver or main cause of my desire to die, the stress didn't help things and continues to be a vulnerable point.

My brain is in a state of foggy mush: everything is going in one ear and out the other. It is partly the anaesthetic. Having been under for so many hours, it would still be coursing through my body, according to the doctors. When I am trying to concentrate, my eyes sting and feel heavy with tiredness. I just can't seem to stay awake or stay focused.

One of today's chores was gathering things I need for study. A wooden stand to hold my textbooks and notes upright. A chair for the desk we've set up in a corner of the house. There is something about the chair. It cost a few hundred dollars and is a serious, grown-up, long-term chair. The type of chair that you would only buy if you were planning to use it for many years. I want it to signify my will to live, but the more I try to force the feeling, the less certain I am.

One beautiful thing about my new study corner is having my computer set up – and music. This year, I've used music like a friend or a conduit for my emotions.

A few songs in particular are echoing my innermost thoughts. 'With or Without You' reminds me of first watching *Looking for Alibrandi*, in which a cover of the U2 song was played when a character suicides. Years later, and not so many months ago from now, I watched the movie again and decided (despite the cliché) it would be my funeral song. The scenes showing everyone's reactions to the suicide made me feel the full power of the pain I knew I would cause others. I remember it slamming into me and tumbling me like seaweed in the surf.

I want to be able to use other people's anticipated pain and grief to help me come back from the suicide precipice, but I am not sure if it just deepens my sadness instead.

I keep trying to study – it helps to be able to talk through my notes while Cécile irons or washes up or gardens. The fluttering anxiety is just below the surface. It feels strange to be planning my exams after I expected not to be alive for them.

Somehow, with study time, bathing, house chores, required shopping and anaesthetic-induced naps in between, the day is gone again and all of a sudden I am back in bed where I started.

Cécile

The morning already has its rituals: conversation in your bed, breakfast, list for the day, bath and hair wash. While bathing you, I pluck up my courage and mention the scars on your thighs.

'Are they recent?'

'Some are, some are very old.'

'Like how old?'

You say you started to cut yourself when you were maybe eight or nine.

My world crumbles again.

You show me old ones.

'How did you do it then?'

'Pocketknife.'

'Pocketknife?'

Do I remember the knives we bought in France? Yes, you were three at the time; I bought all of you your first pocketknives, round blade, each with a different coloured handle. I do remember.

'But we used to go to the beach so often. I never saw anything.'

'Board shorts are great.'

I can picture the photos of you in board shorts, happy on the beach. How old would you have been then? And then I picture young, sweet, gentle you, hurting yourself in your room. How come I never saw blood on your sheets, or pyjamas? This is bad, so bad: me, your mother, oblivious to your deep trouble. Seeing you as the strong one who is always coping.

'And all the holidays at the beach with your friends?'

'It's easy to turn around when you are getting changed.'

So nobody knew. You managed to hide it. Did you ever wish someone would find out and ask?

You still want to take your end-of-the-year exams – as if nothing had happened, or not wanting to feel you have lost a year of hard study. This is the determined, strong-willed Oceane I have misread. We decide to install a study corner for you in the part of the house we still call the play area. All usual precautions about spending money are gone. You need as much spoiling as you desire, if that holds your head above water.

Early afternoon, community mental health calls again:

'How are you doing?'

'Fine.'

'All right, we'll call back on Monday.'

I do not understand. Don't they come and check how you actually are, where you are, if you are looked after properly? You could be telling them any old story, and they would have no idea, no idea. But I suppose, if you kill yourself it will look like they have done their job, according to the rules.

It would be such a relief not to be the only one responsible for your survival.

A bit later that afternoon, I am lying down on my bed with the phone next to me when the community mental health centre near your college calls.

A female voice says: 'We are very concerned that Oceane was discharged from hospital.'

'Yes?'

'Do you realise she should never have been discharged so soon?'

'I don't know. She was, and I promised to look after her. I have taken time off work for that.'

'Well,' says the professional voice, 'you have to know this is a terrible mistake. Do you realise there is a good chance she is going to do it again as soon as she can?'

The terror rushes back through my arteries; I struggle for words. 'Is there something I do not realise and should know about while looking after her? Could you help me?'

'If you had seen her file you would realise she should be in hospital.'

'I haven't seen her file. But you saw her for a while.' *When you would watch her swallow higher and higher doses of antidepressants that only made her puke and gave her vision troubles.* 'Could you help? Can you tell me something?'

'No. Sorry we can't. What we know is confidential, but if you knew what we know ...'

'I don't, I only know that she would have probably killed herself in the psych ward.'

'Well, all I can tell you is to watch her 24/7.'

'She is in her own room at night – is that not right? Should I sleep in her room? She loves having her space there.' *She would not put up with me sleeping in her room. Don't I have to partly trust her so she can have some life of her own?*

'She should not be alone. She could hide something under her mattress during the day and kill herself during the night. We just want to let you know.'

Thank you very much for your very unhelpful help. Thank you for terrifying me even more, to the point I have become totally numb and paralysed.

I put the phone down.

Do they think I am that naive? Am I?

Oceane, I feel strongly that you have a better chance of survival here than being locked up in a hospital. This is the most frightening risk I am taking, but in the end if you are to survive, there has to be love, fierce love and commitment, and enough trust. And if you are going to kill yourself anyway, I would rather that you did it knowing you are loved and at home, not in the cold anonymity of the high-security psychiatric unit.

But I cannot say that to any medical or mental health person. They would be offended and think I was deluded about depression and suicidality.

Isabella, my therapist who I have gone so gratefully back to this week, also thinks you should not have been discharged from the hospital. But she is more gentle with it and ready to help me.

I decide to call the registrar who discharged you. Dr Martin gets paged and returns my call in the late afternoon. He confirms that although you should not be left alone that does not mean I need to be stuck to you 24/7. It is OK that you sleep in your own room. He says just to watch your mood.

But then you did manage to hide your suicidality from everyone.

In the following days we will work out strategies. There will be a carer for you at all times of the day – me or a friend. The baton holder will be responsible for you till they hand over to the next person.

I will trust, even though somewhere in my mind I also know you might be throwing dust in our eyes and waiting for the first opportunity to take your life. *There won't be 'another chance'*, I think to myself. *If she tries again, she will make sure that she does not miss.* That is the reality I am going to have to live with. But meanwhile I'll do everything I can so you know you are loved and I will walk along the precipice with you.

Saturday 9 November 2002

Oceane

Another morning. Another quiet, sleepy start to the day. Me trying to shake off my groggy anaesthetised sleep, and you trying to pry some conversation out of me.

One of the on/off conversations we've had the last few days is about the scars on my thighs. Yesterday Cécile quizzed me in disbelief that I could have done something like that so young. I can't tell if she actually doesn't believe me or if she is just in shock. In the end I feel like I am trying to prove to her that it is true.

The reality is, ninety-five per cent of them are from the last nine months, although there are a few older ones from when I was probably ten or eleven years old. Those episodes were different to the self-hatred and rage I felt this year. Back then, pressing a knife into my body (somehow pressing it in was different to cutting) gave me control. It was like I wanted to give the dysfunctionality of our family and the intangible sadness in the air around Cécile a colour (dark red) and a feeling (sharp) and a smell (salty blood).

But I don't tell Cécile how rarely I cut as a child, or that I wasn't quite as young as what I originally told her – I want her to think it was all the time to make sure she understands how desperate I was and how much the family dynamics hurt me.

Later in the morning, our family friends Alison and Mick come by to take me on my first outing without Cécile. We've agreed that Alison and Mick are designated 'safe' people to be responsible for me. Miranda comes too, and we go down the road to the lake and sit with a picnic by the water. It's peaceful – a glorious change from being inside or in town with everyone staring. Mick and Alison have so much love and warmth, and all without the extra dollop of hurt and pain that I see in the eyes of family. It is so good to laugh and not be asked about details or reasons or justifications for my actions. The heat makes my arms clammy with sweat, but it is strangely intoxicating to be in the sunshine with the smell of gum and a tinge of smoke in the background.

I think Miranda has come down from the City just to give me a drawing she has made – of my two hands, showing gaping open wounds, with a poem written in them.

It is pretty intense – the words and the image – which feels good in a way. I think my emotions at the moment are so exaggerated that I crave things that are equally extreme in order to actually feel them.

I've had a mixed past with Miranda. She was a big reason I moved in with my dad after the separation; she was fun and loving in a way that really boosted me. Her parents, whom I call Oma and Grandpa, and also her sister Mieke, Mieke's husband Hans and their two gorgeous girls Tess and Yarrow, instantly accepted and loved me without question, and have become my 'blown in by the wind' family. Despite her relationship with my dad breaking down this year, I have no doubt that Miranda will stay in my life.

Living with Miranda wasn't always easy: she could be completely self-centred, taking up all the attention with her chronic illness, or completely shutting me down when I was being a normal teenager wanting to listen to music or do my own thing. But when she wasn't caught up in herself, she was amazingly thoughtful. It's been hard not knowing which Miranda I am going to get, the needy or the supportive.

But I knew when I called her on my first night in hospital that she would come with the supportive face on, and that unlike others, I didn't have to think twice about how she would feel or react.

The poem means a lot to me and it is good to have something that acknowledges the sharpness and scarring that is the reality right now. I need this side of Miranda, who can understand what is happening inside me and help me translate it.

Poem from Miranda

You have marked yourself

With sharpness.

Now there is no way

You cannot use the blade

Embedded in the memory

Of your flesh but

To cut the truth from

The heavens;

Our tears hang from that edge.

They say: look into us, we

Are your mirror

Beautiful

Still you are

And we are

Grateful.

Cécile

You are preparing for your first social outing, a picnic. You have managed to put your undies and jeans on by yourself: another bit of autonomy reclaimed. You have chosen a bright summery top and the hessian bag you fell in love with on your first day out of hospital.

After you've gone, I decide to walk to a friend's place for a cup of coffee. We share the suicide of our beautiful children – hers lost not long ago and mine hopefully not.

As I reach the lake on my walk home around lunchtime I gasp: from the back of the mountain, just behind the lake, glowing smoke is billowing. This does not make sense – our fires have always come from the west, not from the east like this one.

These are funny moments when thinking seems to stop and yet goes so fast. *Run home, Cécile, run home, quick. Catch Leon before he leaves to visit Oma and Grandpa in the Capital. Come on, legs, do not wobble, run, run. You can make it. Run all the way home, up the short hill, round the bend, to the house.*

Leon is just driving out, light and self-assured at the wheel of his first car. I wave my arms like a madwoman:

'Leon! Leon!' I shout, 'Stop! Stop!'

He looks perplexed, his joyful trajectory interrupted once more.

'Leon! Bushfire!'

At the word his whole body becomes alert, braced for the emergency.

'Leon, it's just behind the mountain! It looks like it's coming quick. We've got to get the house ready.'

No hesitation. Leon turns his car around and we arrive together at the door. He knows: 'You tell me what to do. You be the boss. Just tell me.'

The list of tasks: block the valves at the water tank, turn the roof sprinklers on, dress for fire, close all windows and draw the curtains, fill the bath up … it all comes out precisely, erasing panic. Speed, efficiency. We've had several fire scares in the past years.

Oceane, this is when I call you. I try to stay calm, putting on my best Australian way for very Australian circumstances:

'Oceane, I don't know if you guys have realised, but there is a bushfire coming. What would you like to do?'

Your breath stops for a second. You too know how to stay calm in the middle of storms.

'I want to come home' – short and clear – 'I am coming home.'

'Sure.'

'Just a second.' I hear your voice over the covered phone. 'I'll be home in ten minutes.'

Oceanette, it is such a reassurance to see you pack the belongings you do not want to lose into boxes and ask Mick and Alison if they would keep these at their place while the fires threaten. At night, after Leon has eventually left for the Capital, hoping all is safe enough, we sit on the veranda and watch the fire reach the ridge of the mountain, slowly coming our way down the hill. For that evening, it feels like the mad destroyer, the raging threat we've been living, has moved outside, threatening our home instead of us.

Sunday 10 November 2002

Oceane

Today is a tough day. Made tougher by the fact that the relief of being out of hospital is wearing off. And there is also an impending exam on Tuesday hanging over me. I have been granted a scribe who will write out all my answers. I try practising with Cécile, speaking out loud answers to questions I make up, but it is not so easy. The words are stuck and sometimes I just want to collapse in a heap and sleep or die.

Cécile asks me, 'Do you still wish it had worked?' I don't know how to answer. I feel as fragile as butterfly wings, and I have moments of soaring, thrilling happiness at the smallest things. I am balancing on a bit of a knife's edge. Yes, I wish it had worked. That is the honest answer, because as I slipped into unconsciousness on that Tuesday night I felt with complete certainty that this was the right thing to do and that the awaited oblivion was the most welcome thing in the world. So yes, part of me won't ever wish that it hadn't worked, because the pain and desperation in me at the time was worthy of death. My 'highs' make it easier to be alive right now in this moment, but they do not cancel out the desperation.

Today, memories of my twenty-four-hour self-destruct sequence haunt me. Swallowing the packets of painkillers and sleeping pills. One by one, slowly, to stop myself gagging. Every time I close my eyes I can see myself holding the razor – hovering it in readiness. Then I can see myself slicing with all my power behind it. I remember the seconds before, worrying that I would chicken out and only cut superficially. I remember my gasp as I see my wrist open up like a mango cheek turning inside out. I remember the surprise and pride at how deep I'd managed to cut – but also my worry that it wasn't deep enough.

Then the plastic bag.

Then slowly feeling the hot, humid darkness of my breath in the bag till oblivion took over and I passed out.

These memories haunt me every time I shut my eyes or quieten my mind too much. The side effect is aversion to pain. I couldn't hurt myself or take my life right now, I am so hyper-sensitised. I cannot imagine even pricking myself with a pin, let alone cutting or tying something around my neck. I have to get away from these images in my head. I can't concentrate on studying for Tuesday with them hovering around. I put on my music – happy, funky dancing music – and that slowly eases me out of the pit of darkness. The music also helps me wake up and I manage to get a bit more study done.

There has been a lot more peace today with Leon gone. It has been hard for me to have him around. He is a reminder of negative memories and difficulties. Not that they all involve him – he was just one cog in the bigger machine of our family, of the fear and frustration, the insecurity and intensity of all those years. Being around any member of the family takes up so much energy for me.

I am early to bed, relieved to escape into the quiet of my room, with my pillows propped around me. I rely on my Discman to put me to sleep. I can't hold a book with my useless arms, but I can listen to stories, and it seems to distract my mind enough to keep the nasty thoughts out until I am asleep.

Cécile

You are lying on the sofa in the lounge and I am sitting by your feet. Yesterday's stress and the heat are flattening our energy. We are safe. The fire has been contained. All windows are open, in the hope that some breeze might come and create a draught to cool us down.

Helicopters are crossing nonstop over our heads, filling up at the lake down the road before flying away heavy with the thousands of litres of water they are throwing at the fires that are raging in the national park – our backyard. It is unnerving, the way they are first just a distant drone and then without warning become the loudest roar that engulfs the whole house, superimposing their own rhythm on the one of our strained conversation.

I am still hoping that I can gently push your mind towards the side of the life–death divide I want you to be on. I don't look at you. Thinking aloud feels like it gives you a bit more space than directing questions at you. I have become acutely aware of any little tensing up in you when I push too much, and yet I cannot help myself.

'You know, Oceane, most people who have tried to kill themselves ... you know ... you know ... most of them, later ...'

Helicopter.

'Later in their life, they say they are glad they didn't die. You know, when they look back at how they didn't want to live and the ...'

Next helicopter.

'And the life they have now ...'

You listen, eyes anchored on a spot on your shorts.

Helicopter.

Silence. Both silent: you taking it in, thinking; me waiting.

Helicopter.

Then you look up with the gaze of someone who is looking inside their head to find their words.

'They would have to say THAT.' My chin lifts as I try to meet your eyes in enquiry.

Helicopter.

'They'd have to say that,' you repeat.

When the helicopter has passed, you offer a bit more:

'They just have to create a reason for not having managed to die.'

You are not going to buy my bullshit.

Monday 11 November 2002

Oceane

I woke earlier than I wanted to this morning, with the same blankness of drugged sleep, even though I haven't had sleeping pills. No indication or proof that I've been asleep when I wake up. No dreams, nothing to tell me what my brain has been doing for all those hours.

We head to the City today, for a visit; I am desperate to see friendly faces and to have the lightness of Ben, Dina and Alice's company. I also need some more lecture tapes and other material for exams.

We hit the road – Cécile looks exhausted. I wonder what you are thinking, Mama, as you concentrate on driving.

The questions come out before we've even reached the highway, and I sense your need to understand what has happened. Make the links. We flitter over childhood memories – ones of the family fighting, your depression and tears.

I can't give you the information you need to be reassured. It is not that I don't want to, not that I want you to struggle with this uncertainty and be so fearful. It's not too late or anything dramatic like that, but it is not within my ability to divulge, to share, to nut through the tangled mess of my thoughts with you. I have never been able to talk about this with you – we've never had the ease of communicating about these things. The entrenched habit between us is that I stay silent, strong, quiet in case I become the tipping point that makes *you* suicide, or leave the family, or completely collapse to a point of no return.

I know you are no longer fragile in that way and that you desperately want to be there for me. But it's hard to forget, Cécile. It is hard to forget those mornings when I'd go into the bathroom to find you sobbing in the shower. Or when I'd be about to leave for school but then would stay to console you as you cried and told me you could not handle it anymore, that you'd had enough. In these memories I am five or six years old. I knew from that age what suicide was and I worried you would commit suicide. That isn't right for a five-year-old. I wasn't meant to be your support. The weight silenced me. I knew too much about you, Cécile, not even just your sadness in the moment: I knew you had been raped, I knew your family had shamed you and mistreated you and that you had lived in fear. I was too young to know what to do with that information and so I just grew up thinking I had to protect you from anything that might make you more sad or make you acknowledge that I too was now growing up with shame and fear.

I'm so focused on these horrible memories, but I want to do justice to the positive stories as well. Tell you that I loved our camping holidays and that having no TV as kids made us creative and adventurous and healthy. Why can't I tell you about how much I loved our trip to France to see our cousins? The pleasure in eating cheese and bread bought fresh at the markets, the feeling of connectedness to these cousins from newborn to forty years old, as we all played a massive game of soccer on the front lawn of Grandmère's house. The happy stories are as stuck in my head as the sad stories, and yet I can't share either with you.

I am relieved when we arrive at college. Alice, Ben and Dina come out and meet me and I feel carried by them as we meander through the hallways to Alice's room. I have butterflies in my tummy until we are safely ensconced there – desperate not to run into anyone.

I sit on Alice's bed. Among my safe little cocoon of friends I can finally speak honestly and articulately. It's as if now that my secret is out, I am no longer muted, but can converse normally. We talk about books, college gossip, who knows what else. It doesn't matter because I feel completely high. Like when I walked out of hospital free, I can see every colour, every flash of sunlight, every object with a new pair of eyes. I am nearly dissociated from my body – floating above this little room of chatting and laughing teenagers. So this is what life is meant to feel like.

Half an hour later there is a knock on the door and Bonnie – who I haven't seen since she took me to hospital – comes in.

She has been looking for me. I don't know what to say. It is so awkward after the last time I saw her: rushing to hospital, dealing with my admission, hearing her speak on my behalf to the triage nurse, doctors, and the community mental health centre people. In the back of my mind I've wondered what she thinks of me. Why she hasn't been to see me.

Bonnie is not here for a friendly chat. Something is up and she needs a quiet word with me. My heart sinks. Does she have bad news for me? Has Cécile had an accident? My biggest fear is that somehow they've convinced someone to force me back to hospital.

Bluntly, Bonnie explains to me that I am not welcome at the college – I've been kicked out.

I become fixated on these words and the tears come fast. I have never been in trouble in my life really. Never been told I am not welcome. Never been in detention at school, suspended, let alone expelled from anywhere.

I am in shock – not even embarrassed to be crying, although I know the shame will hit me later.

She tells me they have packed up my room. They didn't even ask me first. The thought of them going through my belongings, reading my notes, seeing my personal things, makes my skin crawl. Who packed my stuff? What did they say to each other as they did? What did they do with the bloodstains? The complete disregard for my personal space is another violation, another boundary inappropriately crossed.

She tells me that the dean was told by a doctor at the hospital that I'd be unlikely to survive. Slimy excuse. Were they that keen to get rid of me that they didn't even wait the three days the doctor apparently gave me, to find out if I would live or not?

I learn from Bonnie about how upsetting this has been for other students. Are they talking about Ben, Dina and Alice, who I told myself? Are my friends upset and not telling me? Or have they told others? Where is my privacy in all this? Where is my control over my life and personal story? When do I get consulted? It is suddenly clear that Bonnie has been sent as the messenger – she appears kind and youthful and compassionate but she is part of the college. Not here as my friend and certainly not here as a support.

I hate that the college have gone behind my back. Telling others of my most shameful and private moments. It is the same feeling I had in the psych ward, of having no autonomy. The same with the local community mental health centre team: they just made decisions for me about starting medication and there was no sense of being a human with my own opinion or thoughts about that. Now it is happening here. People told, decisions made, things done without asking me. Without caring what I want or how it makes me feel.

There is a tone in Bonnie's words that suggests this is all my fault. 'The repercussions of my actions.' Like I deserve this after what I have done. It is hard not to just nod and believe it.

Cécile and I leave after that – it is clear just how unwelcome we are. But my Taurean gumption kicks in and I defiantly text the others to meet me on the university lawn just metres away from college, where they have no control over me.

The huge low of the talk with Bonnie doesn't stay with me, thankfully. I swing back into what I am starting to think of as my 'post-suicidal high', or my 'suicide rebound', sitting on the grass in the green skirt I made last year, in the fabric that I love – it makes me feel fresh and springlike. My arms are still in their heavy plaster, but not hurting as much.

We spend the afternoon talking on the lawn, making future plans. Getting a house together next year. Sharing the cooking and cleaning. Philosophising, entertaining, studying. Getting out of college, which we are all desperate to do. It is obviously a necessity for me now that I've been kicked out.

But perhaps I am secretly relieved to be expelled. I needed the decision made for me. All year I've been spiralling down in this environment – terrorised by Seth and the memory of fighting him off – but I couldn't leave. I was trapped by my reliance on Angie and Bonnie, and what I realise was a false sense of friendship, and my financial reliance on the part scholarship and the work I could do for the college in exchange for some of my fees. By the time it was obvious that the environment was killing me – nearly literally – I didn't have the strength to get out.

Now, the possibilities seem endless.

I am so thrilled by the future house plans. I feel enveloped in security and warmth. And maybe, just maybe it is more than the post-suicide high. Is this what life could be like? Is this sense of connection and belonging a glimpse of what I could feel every day? I have a moment of thinking maybe I could do this life thing if it felt like this more often.

Cécile

I drop you at the college car park. Your friends appear and sweep you off, leaving behind only a trail of joyful giggles.

As I drive off the man who had introduced himself to me as the dean of the college on the previous Tuesday stops my car. I pull up and roll my window down.

'Hello,' I say in a friendly way.

'You have brought Oceane?'

'Yes, she's come to visit her friends.'

'And who is looking after her?'

'It's all been arranged. She will be staying with her friends all the time and they'll SMS me to come and pick her up.'

'I am not very happy about that,' he mutters. 'Would you come to my office, please?'

'Sure, I'll just park the car.'

I go in. The receptionist tells me the dean will be with me shortly.

Yes indeed, he arrives and with reinforcements.

He introduces me to another middle-aged man. The master. I am also introduced to Bonnie. Ah this is Bonnie ... I am so happy to meet her. I like her straight away. The roundness of her face conveys to me a sense of warmth and gentleness.

'We are not very happy about Oceane visiting,' declares the dean.

'Oh!'

'It is not good.'

'Oh, I am surprised. We did this last week. She loves seeing her friends.'

'Well, actually she has been dismissed from this college. As a matter of fact, she is not allowed on these grounds.'

'What!' I fumble for words. 'But, we haven't been told. This is the first time I am hearing this.'

'That's right, we haven't let you know yet.'

Oceane, I am starting to really understand how you have been feeling. More and more let down by all the people who said they were there for you. I am not ready for a battle. The image of you and your joy at spending time with your friends lingers in my mind.

'This is going to be so upsetting for Oceane. I am seeing her at lunchtime. I guess I will have to let her know then.'

'Sorry, I don't think you understand. She is not allowed on these grounds. You understand? She is not allowed on these grounds now.'

'What! But we had no idea. We haven't been told and we've come all the way for her to visit her friends. She's been looking forward to this morning so much. Surely, she can have her morning here today and then we'll work something out.'

'Sorry.' Such finality. 'It is not like that. You have to understand, this has been very … very … disturbing for the students. They are just starting their exams. We've had to tell them what's happened and some of them have been very, very upset. We have to look after our students, as we are sure you would appreciate.'

Oh yes, you dismiss Oceane and you don't have to look after her anymore. I like your Christian logic.

'Oceane is no longer a member of our college and she has to go now.'

'But, you cannot do that. You cannot disappoint her so suddenly. She's just come home from hospital and we've had bushfires close to our home all weekend. She is extremely fragile. This is dangerous for her.'

I look towards Bonnie, sure she understands. Sure she is going to intervene for you. She is your friend. Bonnie looks at me and smiles, yet says nothing.

By that stage, I am in tears – struck again by fear, shock, disbelief, frustration and powerlessness. Their condescending smiles and false concern as they push a box of tissues towards me sickens me.

'Sorry.' They look to Bonnie, who has remained silent through our conversation. 'Bonnie, do you know where Oceane is? Would you go and find her, please?'

'Yes sure.'

Bonnie gets up. How can she? She is a traitor.

They leave me there alone.

After half an hour Bonnie arrives with you. You too have been crying. I feel so angry. I despise them all.

Bonnie leaves us.

'Oceanette, I cannot believe this is happening.'

'They have emptied my room ... there is nothing left there.'

'This is terrible. Let's get out of here.'

We walk to the car. Within fifteen minutes you and your real friends have arranged to meet on the uni grounds. Blessings to mobile phones. You turn to me with a cheeky smile: 'After all, I am banished from college only, not from uni.'

Hurrah! They haven't broken your spirit; they cannot stop you. Spending the afternoon with your friends is spiced with the excitement of rebellion. While I am waiting at a cafe at the shopping centre my mobile phone beeps: 'Am having such a great time – can we meet a bit later?'

When we get back home in the afternoon, there has been no word from community mental health.

Tuesday 12 November 2002

Oceane

Exam today. The suspense is sitting in my belly.

Life is so volatile. I can feel the depth and darkness of gloom nearby. It is physical, a hard edge in my mind that I feel I can touch. I sense that if I fall into it, there will be no return. Luckily though, I can make sure I don't stray too close, although sometimes it takes every trick in the book. I have to promise myself things, coax myself, distract myself like a child with a toy. It wasn't so long ago that I was in that hell, and I know what it will mean to go back there. The next time there will be no errors, so I make sure not to get too close. I ask Cécile for a new pretty thing, or I listen to a song. Anything to stop myself falling.

My focus today though is my first exam. It feels too soon, but the only thing worse than having to sit an exam with my foggy brain and useless arms is the thought of dragging out the exams any longer. I need to be done by the end of the year. Prolonging the anticipation will only bring me towards the perilous edge.

The test is biology, and I have enough interest in the subject to be able to cope, although speaking my answers to the scribe is awful. We get home and I am beyond exhausted.

Leon is back from his time visiting Oma and Grandpa in the Capital. He is back in his element. Any shyness or uncertainty he had from jetlag and the chaos he arrived into is well and truly gone and he is once again the king of the castle. Loud music, loud conversations, teasing, mocking, needling. He is bursting the bubble that I felt I was creating with Cécile. The slow rhythm, the trust, the conversations. Although not easy, we were getting ourselves synched with each other – but now Leon is here, jarring, disrupting, taking energy that is precious to me at the moment.

I want to leave Cécile's, get away from him, but I don't know where I'd go. I don't know what to do, but I worry that Leon will be a tipping point into the abyss.

Cécile

I drive you to your first exam in the crispy early morning, the rising sun blinding us on the highway already packed with commuters' cars. You explain to me how you have not wanted to push yourself to study during the past week, so as not to become depressed again.

'I have to have enough good things to keep my head above water or I will drown,' you add matter-of-factly.

My stomach churns. I don't think I can provide more good things and yet I am just keeping you afloat, just. What if I fail, just a bit? You are not aware that I have no money left. Am I bound to fail you? It scares me.

Wednesday 13 November 2002

Oceane

I woke up this morning knowing that I needed to do something physical with my body – yoga. I need to feel alive in my arms, legs, muscles, bones. I am craving the sensation of stretching, pushing myself, movement. I called around and found a studio that will do a lesson with me. Yes! I am euphoric to have this to look forward to.

The harder conversation this morning was about Leon – when I woke up I also knew what I had to do there. It has to be me or him. I can't share this space at the moment. I know it is completely selfish of me, but I need to feel like I am the priority.

I have asked you to choose between two of your children, and I can see how painful it is for you, Cécile. It is incredibly hard, telling you what I need.

Your children have never quite stopped being at war with each other – but we saw the same between you and Oliver in your separation. I can't forget all the negativity and slander. You were both equally guilty of it – trying to influence us kids, accusing each other to serve your own purpose. I can tease apart some of the truths from the lies, but in the end all the stories made me mistrustful of both of you.

My weakness has been – and still is – my need to protect others' feelings. It is what I have always done with the family. It became important for me to try and fix everything.

For some reason I always felt the most enormous and oppressing sense of responsibility for Oliver's happiness in particular. I needed to be his supportive, loving daughter, his confidante. When I saw Oliver sad or suffering with stress – during the separation from you, the custody battles, or later the divorce from Miranda – I felt it acutely in my body. It was worse than any emotional distress that I ever felt for myself at the time. I don't know why it was so strong, but it was, and it made me act quickly to repair it because I couldn't cope with the depth of my empathy for Oliver.

My need to protect you has been more subtle. Your need, according to my five-year-old analysis of the situation, was for an easy, compliant child who didn't create any more problems. I couldn't fix anything for you, Cécile, but I could make sure not to exacerbate anything. I could make sure that at least with me, you would never have to expend energy chastising or fighting. I remember the one time you raised your voice at me I was absolutely devastated. I must have been seven years old, maybe eight, and I'd excitedly rushed in after school one afternoon. You were drinking a hot black coffee as you always did, I still remember the smell of it on your breath, and I bumped you as I climbed into your lap, causing your coffee to spill. You were more surprised than angry, but made some sort of exclamation about being careful and calming down and how hot the coffee was. This tiny sign that I had caused you some sort of issue – a momentary hassle – reduced me to tears for hours.

So now, years down the track, at my most vulnerable and fragile, I am allergic to the hurt and needs of others. I can feel the pull of the trap – it would be so easy to take on your desperation, but I know that for self-preservation, I need to stay firm.

Leon leaves, and I go and hide in my room, feeling the shame and trying to push away the distress.

Cécile

You are lying on the sofa. As I approach to ask you if you need anything, you hiss through your clenched teeth:

'It's me or him.'

'What?'

'If Leon does not go, I am going.'

What is going on? You or him? Impossible. Leon has just returned from Europe. He needs a transition time and also to digest the shock. Besides, he has been amazingly helpful. Sure, he has become more noisy in the last few days, often playing his music loudly. Sure, he can be in your face at times, a great teaser. He's just being a nineteen-year-old.

But what choice do I have?

'Leon, I am sorry.'

'It's OK, Cécile. Don't worry, I'll go.'

'I am sorry, Leon.'

My heart hurts.

Later that night, after Leon has left the Mountains to stay with friends in the City he calls: 'Oceane has to be our priority. I am not angry at her for saying I had to go. I understand. I was overstaying and you two had to give me the push. No bad feelings.'

'Thank you, Leon. I love you.'

'I know, don't worry.'

The air is starting to cool down. Still no word from community mental health. Looks like they have forgotten you.

Thursday 14 November 2002

Cécile

Today I am seeing my first clients after two weeks off. Having to dress for work and be in my office puts some normality back into my life. Although I normally like my job, today I have no inclination to see my clients. I do not really want to hear about people's depression, suicidal thoughts and other miseries that seem so petty. The thought keeps crossing my mind: I'd rather be able to help my daughter than all these people. But I need to earn some money and maintain my practice. I am dreading the first contact, my client's concerned look or curiosity about what happened. When they ask if my child is OK and I say yes, she'll be fine. I feel like a liar.

Friday 15 November 2002

Oceane

I am wired for my first trip to the psychiatrist today. It is a lady that a colleague of Cécile recommended. Apparently she is an expert in adolescent psychiatry – I'll be happy just as long as she is better than the changing guards at the hospital. My hope is that surely she can't be worse.

Cécile and I drive to the City, as usual slipping into the big conversations as we merge onto the highway heading out of town. There is something quite relaxing about the rhythm of the highway – the white lines flashing past, the drone of the car. It's always been a good time for me to ask Cécile big questions about her life. Occasionally I've even found myself sharing something. We get there with plenty of time to spare. We seem to be already well practised at the drive to the City.

I wait nervously in the waiting room till I'm called. Cécile continues to wait for me, always there in the background. On days like today it isn't so bad: supportive, not oppressive.

My previous experience of the therapy world leaves much to be desired. First there were the family sessions when I was seven or eight with a therapist who left us in long, awkward silences. The odd times that we spoke, it would often end with angry explosions. The police were even called once, mid therapy. I, as always, sat in silence and didn't say a word. I would think to myself, 'Why won't anyone ask how I am doing?' After a year or so of all those drives to the City and missed school days, there was no change and we stopped going.

Years later, we tried family therapy again with a psychologist. The only good memory of that was getting to leave school early every Wednesday and the delicious falafels for dinner afterwards.

Earlier this year, I tried two counsellors as I felt myself spiral downwards. The first was clearly out of her depth with me. She was a student psychologist, so it was free, and I didn't feel she even knew where to start. She told me perhaps I needed to find someone more experienced.

The second was cheap too, ten dollars, which fitted in my budget, but by session two, it was obvious that she was determined to make me believe that God could help me, and that I should consider seeking his salvation. As an atheist from childhood, for me this was the worst possible solution that anyone could suggest. I remember thinking, 'If you think that God is the only hope for me, then I am truly screwed.'

The final chapter in my therapy experience, my recent week in hospital, actually made me feel more suicidal than when I'd arrived. At least I left on a good note with Dr Martin.

The first session with Dr Robert is easy. Other than a bit of shyness on my part, it is straightforward, covering the basic information that has brought me here. It feels easy because it is simply facts and events.

I describe my year: moving to the City to start uni and moving into a college; the assaults and attempted rape by Seth; then the months of trauma associated with still seeing Seth, being harassed by him. I tell her of the downward spiral, turning to cutting and eventually my final decision and suicide attempt.

There is something strengthening in the seriousness with which Dr Robert attends to my story. I tell her of my hesitancy about therapy – how I find it hard if there is too much silence in a session and that I need to be asked questions to be able to share information. She listens with a small smile on her lips and when the hour is up I leave feeling OK. I am a little nervous of all that is to come in terms of divulging and working on myself, but hope that I will get there. There is a sense that I am 'performing' for her, but I think that mostly stems from my anxiety about being scheduled and my fear that saying the wrong thing might force me back into hospital.

Later that day, I have my first yoga lesson. The studio

is tucked upstairs in a big hall, with wooden floorboards and beautiful candles, flowers and energy.

The teacher clearly wonders why I have two arms in plaster. He is burning with curiosity and I can sense he is trying to get the story from me without overstepping professional boundaries. I stick with what feels safe to me: 'I had an accident.' But I am acutely aware of just how non-accidental it really was.

There is obviously not much I can do with zero use of my hands, but he is creative and a very good teacher, and I leave after an hour feeling strong, lean, and alive; my post-suicidal high is in full swing.

Despite the positivity of therapy and yoga, at the end of the day a volcano erupts between Cécile and me. It is not a new phenomenon – it has built up over years of financial worry, anxiety, neediness and expectations – but it is the first time it explodes with such ferocity.

Cécile has made a bill. A list of all the charges she has incurred looking after me. It is every cent that she has spent on me, whether I've asked for it or not. She has even put down the tolls she paid visiting me in hospital. I nearly want to laugh. There are the costs of drinks, bandages, plastic shower gloves, even the masking tape to wrap the gloves around my arms.

So this is what caring for me is like for her. A long list of costs. How can this even be on her mind? Suddenly the intensity of her love, worry, nurturing is cheapened.

If it is such a burden for you, Cécile, why don't you just fuck off and let me fend for myself?

I can't believe my own harshness, but she has no idea how hurtful it is to see every moment we've had together in the last two weeks priced to the cent.

Cécile looks terrified by my anger. I can see her helplessness and, eventually, her worries about financial security. We end the day wary, shaking with many layers of unspoken stories and fears. This is just one of the family burdens I've carried since I was a child. I was always aware of our financial predicament, from literal homelessness as a baby and young child to years of restrictive diet, constantly overhearing stressed conversations or petty post-separation bickering about child support. I know as immigrants and with little family support, you did it tough, Cécile, but I don't want to feel responsible for it. I'm sick of carrying your financial woes.

Cécile

Driving you to your first therapy appointment, I so much hope this will be a place for you to heal and find your way back to life, to yourself, to realising what a beautiful person you are.

After the appointment, I have to do some work. It's a difficult day: juggling seeing my clients, supervision and driving you to and from safe friends' houses, to and from yoga class, all the time wondering how you are going.

'Yoga is fantastic,' you declare with a grin as you hop in the car after your class.

But later I mess up, Oceane, and I will be so sorry for it.

Earlier, your father had called and asked me to pay half of a dentist bill for Julian. I let loose:

'Do you know how much I have spent on Oceane?'

'No I don't. Let me know and I'll contribute,' he replied.

Well, did I let him know. I put down everything. Not only the medical costs, but the food and drinks and treats and clothes and petrol for the many journeys, the lot. I left the sheet of paper on my desk – which I thought was a private space – and you found it, Oceane. And you felt I had resented every bit I had given to you and you were so upset.

It was terrifying to see you so angry, and once more feeling not really loved, but a load on your parents. No 'sorry' on my part could repair the mess. You closed off, would not talk to me, and I was left in dread you might turn your anger against yourself once more.

Saturday 16 November 2002

Oceane

My beautiful horse, Freya – who I think of so often, but who has also caused me so much worry – is off in a few days to a new home, and this morning I asked Cécile to take me to see her. We drove up to her paddock and by some miracle she came when I whistled for her. Probably expecting her dinner, but it had the benefit of making me feel very loved.

She tickled her nose across my casts, searching for a carrot. I apologised to her for pinning the blame of my two casts on her. She is in the throes of her adolescence: wilful, self-righteous, telling me she is completely entitled to all the love, attention and food which I bring her. She squeals at her paddock mates when they come too close – defending her carrots zealously and with the confidence that comes from being in her prime.

I felt so alive from having the smooth dirty grey fingertips that only seem to come from horses. I noticed how heightened my senses were to the smell of horsehair, chewed hay and dust. Cécile took photos and later when we print them, they are so romantic, black and white, grainy. The slender girl whispering to her horse.

This evening, tentatively balanced between the joy of my outing to see Freya and the empty grief from our argument yesterday, Cécile and I begin to talk of my suicidality. I try to describe to Cécile how physical the pain felt. How desperate I was to end my suffering and how unbearable life had become. She tells me that if I truly feel there is no other choice, and we've exhausted all options, she would rather help me die peacefully than have me violently end my life alone.

A weight is lifted off my shoulders. I clutch on to those words with every ounce of my being. Finally an option that is bearable. I could do it without huge pain and suffering. I could do it without aloneness and shame.

We don't stay on the conversation long. The enormity of what Cécile is offering hits so deeply that I cannot really speak.

Cécile

We are both tired from yesterday. You are sleeping in so I grab the opportunity to go to the garden while it is cool.

My vegie garden is my refuge. I started growing vegetables in France. I was living in a tiny village on the edge of the Massif Central and teaching at a nearby high school. I had become involved in leftist movements and had recently returned from an antinuclear demonstration.

I was devastated at the violence I had witnessed and at the idea that my own brother was part of the army and police force, responding to provocations from a minute group of troublemakers by using so much force that a number of demonstrators had come out badly maimed. *From now on*, I promised myself, *I will promote life by growing vegetables instead of attending protests.* Since then my kitchen garden has always been a wonderful leveller, especially in times of trouble.

After you wake up, we quietly run through the morning rituals, moving between the exercise bicycle and lecture notes, fighting heat and tiredness, blowflies and mozzies.

When we get back from visiting Freya we sit on the deck with a cool drink, watching the setting sun give the mountain in front of us a soft, warm glow. You say you have been thinking a lot about our conversation earlier this evening – when I said that if at any time you really felt that you could not live anymore, I'd rather help you go gently and with someone who loves you than have you do it with violence and in utter loneliness.

You look at me and ask, 'Do you really mean it?'

I stay quiet for a while. Oceane, this promise was one of the most difficult things to tell you.

'Yes, I mean it, although I dearly hope that you'll never go there again. I am first going to do all I can to help you regain hope and find your yes to life.'

I think of this poem by Jacques Prévert:

Notre père qui êtes aux cieux
Restez-y
Et nous
Nous resterons sur terre

Our father who dwells in heaven
You stay there
And we
We will stay here on earth

Odile, my dearest sister, and I used to read this poem and many others by Prévert aloud, time and time again. Cuddled on my bed that was our refuge from the family. She did not stay on earth. I stayed, and you, my children, were part of my yes to life.

Sunday 17 November 2002

Oceane

I am slowly regaining my independence – it is such sweet relief! The trust has built up. I think Cécile must know that because she has offered to support me in suicide if I truly need to, I won't sneak off and do it alone. And I can accept that – I won't kill myself behind her back. Not if she truly means she would help me if it came to that.

I head off, first time driving on my own. I can only just manage in her automatic car, changing from park to reverse to drive using my slightly stronger right hand. My left hand is useless and has to just rest lightly on the wheel, pretending to participate. I visit an old horseriding friend. The drive is probably the highlight. Playing my music loudly, singing at the top of my lungs to Simon and Garfunkel. Filled with the same excitement I had when I got my Ps and could finally drive myself places.

It makes me think of my time in the Capital. Getting my Ps and revelling in the adventures that I could now have.

It was a big move, but one I'd dreamt of for a long time. My friend Jaz and I had talked about it from year 8 –

it was like this magic dream – moving to the Capital, where the public school system allowed you to have continuous assessment over the last two years of school instead of the dreaded final exams that I was already anxious about.

Jaz and I had instantly bonded in year 7; we were quirky and different to the rest of the kids – Jaz with her dreadlocks and 'don't care' attitude and me with my more goody-two-shoes approach to life. We balanced each other out somehow.

Miranda, who was twenty-four and had just married my dad, had done her last two years at a college in the Capital and made it sound so perfect. Jaz and I, in our thirteen-year-old mightiness, had made intricate plans of how we'd convince our parents to let us go. I don't think either of us really believed it would happen, but when I found myself lost in the war my parents were waging against each other, unable to continue living with either of them, then the escape plan was perfect.

I think Cécile was used to me coming home and announcing things, and just knew not to argue about the move. I was lucky Miranda was on my side – she was an ally in many ways – and talked Oliver into supporting me too. Even better, when Jaz's mum learnt that my parents were letting me go, she let Jaz move up too. So I, fifteen years old, moved in with Leon, and she moved into the boarding house across the road.

We were so smug about our escape from our boring old high school and our sophisticated college life in the Capital. Once I'd gotten my licence over a year later, we'd jump in my beaten-up, ancient green car ('Myrtle the Turtle') and just drive. The Capital became a beautiful place behind the windscreen of that car, spluttering up hills and around endless roundabouts. The cheap Turkish bread and dip we picked up at the markets tasted even more delicious in the picnic spot we were able to drive ourselves to. Driving Cécile's car feels similarly euphoric. I sense the post-suicidal high making the grass greener, the air through the window purer, the setting sun exquisitely vibrant.

Monday 18 November 2002

Cécile

It promises to be a stinking hot day. You are driving to see Freya off. The final decision has been to give her to friends of your adoptive family near the Bay – they have offered to pay to transport her up north, relieving you of your stress about what to do with her. The pain, though, is shrinking your face: the pain of the mother who is not able to keep looking after her little one. You try to be strong, courageous, probably for Freya, and I try to muster enough energy to get through the day – nine clients, no break.

At lunchtime we manage fifteen minutes together, in which you announce that you have a job interview tomorrow at 2 pm at the local shopping centre. Artificial lights, air conditioning, loud music.

Only yesterday we agreed that you would not work next year, just study and live and get better. It made perfect sense to both of us.

You will soon be embarking into your second year at uni; you also intend to enrol in a two-evening-a-week course in sign language, plus practise yoga intensively, plus go to therapy, plus, plus, plus ... Why are you taking a job? Are you frightened you might find yourself having a few free moments?

'No way. Oceane!' I exclaim, though I know it is too late. Your set face tells me you won't shift. No time to discuss more; I need to get back to my afternoon clients.

By the time I have finished with my last client, made a few calls, fed us and Alison and Mick, who have spent the afternoon with you, and they have finally left, it's almost 10 pm. The air is cooling, and we are both heavy with exhaustion, silent.

'What about tomorrow?' I attempt.

You say you have to take the job unless you are guaranteed financial support next year. I feel cornered. Give me some time, please, Oceane; right now I do not have a cent left and will have to manage the summer with very little work.

'Sounds like a bit of blackmail,' I stupidly blurt out.

I should have known it was your anxiety about money and having what you need. Even Leon, who has been keeping in touch and visiting occasionally, pointed this out on the phone last night: 'Oceane is too anxious about money.' I understand why – but I am sorry, Oceane, I did not manage to protect you from that either.

Tuesday 19 November 2002

Oceane

Another day, another trip to the City.

It is harder going through our routine today, after our upset yesterday. As usual, Cécile runs me a bath, just a couple of inches of water. When I'm ready she connects the cheap white shower attachment and hoses off my back – giving it a bit of a scrub with the old horsehair glove bought in France.

But there is a hostility in our morning which is usually so peaceful. I want to scream at Cécile for not understanding my situation – and for her comment about blackmail. That word is so ugly. I don't know what else to do – I need to know that I will be able to live next year – the money has to come from somewhere, and I don't understand how I am supposed to feel secure if Cécile won't accept me working.

I don't expect her to support me. Being independent is one of my greatest sources of strength and pride. Plus I know she can't – but if she is so insistent about me not working then she needs to offer another solution rather than just accuse me of blackmail. I feel set up to fail – not supported and not allowed to support myself.

I can dress myself now at least. I grab my new favourite bag and we are off on the familiar road, this time with a cloud hanging between us.

Cécile

In the middle of the rush to get ready to go to your appointment at the hand clinic, I manage to apologise for the accusation of blackmail. Tears well up in your eyes.

'It was not very nice.' We have a long drive ahead and we'll talk then. Concurrent with my sorry is a scream inside me: 'Oceane, don't do this to me; I am doing my best.' I do not know what to do with that scream. I am constantly afraid that it might escape and create havoc.

The peace comes back as we drive along the highway. We manage to sketch a picture in which your needs will be met. Enough to reassure you for the moment.

I ask you if you know when you started being so anxious about money. 'When I got my first horse and Oliver said I had to be fully responsible for it.'

I wish I could have helped at the time. I was struggling. So my contribution was to drive you to your new horse, back and forth, forth and back, and help you clean the stables on Saturday mornings. I cherished that time with you.

Oceane

We head to the hospital – my first check-up since being discharged. I spend the car trip focusing on my rising worry about going back. I don't want to see Dr C, or any of the psychiatrists, lest they manage to lock me up again.

In between my worry is my pride that I've proved them wrong – I haven't killed myself. Cécile and I have done so well. Cécile has told me snippets of conversations she had with them in the first week of me being home. Telling her that I should never have been released. That I wouldn't be safe. That she wouldn't manage to look after me. I feel triumphant – and nearly want to see those people just to say, 'Ha! Told you I was OK to be released. Look how much better I am.'

The appointment is over in minutes. A bit of an anticlimax. They just needed to check for infection and that things were healing. I tell them of the strange sensations I get. The tingling, pins and needles, numbness and the sense that my hand is swelling and shrinking with my breath. It is apparently all normal with the nerve repair process. I can shut my eyes and instantly see myself cutting into my wrists, destroying my nerves – but I can't seem to picture the healing. Every time I try to visualise the regrowth or the repair, all I can see is my blade poised and then my destruction.

Then I have a few hours of much-needed time with Ben, Dina and Alice. We meet as usual on the little lawn by the creek that separates the college, where I am forbidden, from the university, where I am free.

The conversation turns quickly to something that has been bothering me a lot since being told that I wasn't welcome at college anymore. While I was in hospital, Alice had told me that those considered to be my close friends at college were called into a special meeting and told what I had done. Now, I want to know what was said, how it happened, who was there.

They fill me in. All the girls living in my block and those designated my friends (how did they make that decision?) from other blocks were called into the little apartment belonging to the residential heads, the couple charged with the care of the fifty-odd students in my block. Angie, the floor warden from my block, was also there, and Bonnie of course.

The residential heads explained to the curious group why the meeting had been called. Alice said it was all very solemn – not too different to a wake or a funeral. They explained the seriousness of my attempt and the fact that I was still in emergency in a precarious state. That it wasn't certain I would survive.

Alice described the reactions: some girls cried, some sat in stunned silence. Some looked awkward and uncomfortable. Some wouldn't have even known my name or noticed that I was no longer around. Why were they all told?

Alice, Ben, Dina and a few others that I was close to stayed on for hours apparently. Processing the news, asking questions. Alice sounded a bit proud that she, Ben and Dina had already seen me before this meeting – they were the experts.

It is rare that anyone gets to experience the effect their death would have. At the time that everyone was told, the college's information was that I was unlikely to survive. I feel like a voyeur, a peeping tom, peering into the strange world created by my actions and the ripple-on effect.

I hunger for more details. I want to know every word said, every emotion that flittered across people's faces. They can't report enough detail to settle my panicked mind. I need to know exactly what was said. I crave the details even though it hurts me to hear them. Do I just want to inflict emotional pain on myself or is it helping me realise life is worth living?

I hate this sense of having the most intimate and personal moments of my life bandied around and discussed by others. It is partly a control thing. But there is also so much shame and embarrassment associated with my attempt that when it washes over me, it brings me closer to the abyss of darkness in my mind. I know that to reduce my shame, and avoid that abyss, I need to make sure that I am the one telling the story – explaining it to people in my words. I need people to understand that it wasn't a cry for help; that my failure to commit suicide wasn't because of a lack of trying.

But despite my shame and anger at this breach of privacy, there is something strengthening in the simple fact that people care.

Thursday 21 November 2002

Oceane

I have so much more control over my hands. No strength, but I can type with two fingers and move the mouse. Freedom.

I research on the computer and find out that this post-suicidal high that I've been feeling actually does exist. The literature speaks of euphoria and a heightened sense of the world. It seems similar to the high that some people feel when they've survived an impossible accident or catastrophe. But I was the catastrophe. I gave myself the near-death experience, and now I have the euphoric high.

But unlike what I've read about other survivors of near-death experiences, I am now strangely risk averse. Others, I read, often lose their fear and take up extreme or risky behaviours. I have a deep internal desire to be safe and pain free in every aspect of my day now.

So great is this aversion to any sort of pain that I find myself googling pain-free ways to die. I read about Philip Nitschke, and I wonder if he would respond to an email or if I could purchase some Nembutal online. It is not that

I feel suicidal right this minute, it is just in case – I'd like a security blanket.

Most of all, I fear returning to the hospital system, where I feel I was treated like a criminal: unsafe, invisible, an inconvenience to some and an undeserving bit of scum to others. That week still haunts me: the coldness of some of the doctors and nurses; the sneering remarks; the ever-changing psychiatrists coming in once or twice a day with their never-changing questions.

I can feel the black line drawn through my brain, marking the happy half and the hopeless half. I can feel the endorphins and the pleasure in everyday things at the moment, but I know what the other side is like. I need to know that if I return to it, I have an option: a way out.

Friday 22 November 2002

Oceane

Final exam. Such relief. Linguistics, with most answers short or long essay form. My scribe for this last exam is an older woman. Again, I fight off the curious stares and the subtle questioning. I have no interest in telling her why my arms are like this; I just want the exam over and done with.

I have my second appointment with Dr Robert today too. This one is harder than the first because the preliminaries are over and done with and I get the sense that we are supposed to be starting the 'real work'.

As much as I hated being asked for our family structure at each psychiatric interview in the hospital, I've now realised that it is at least easy to say how many siblings I have. But now that I get to see the same person more than once, I am expected to move on to the bigger stuff. The harder stuff.

I talk a bit about the recurring and intrusive thoughts of my suicide attempt. Dr Robert is the only person I can really get the words out to; I think it would be too distressing for Cécile or any other family members or friends to hear the details. I do occasionally worry that it will be too distressing for Dr Robert as well; I don't know if she really wants to hear it or whether she is too polite to stop me. But giving voice to the images and the details of my attempt feels good, and I hope that it will stop them haunting me every time I close my eyes and try to quieten my mind. I am aware that it is easier to talk about the physicality of my attempt than the tangle of thoughts, emotions and feelings locked in my head.

I am relieved about my exams being over. With that stress finally gone I feel like I can look forward to something else in the future.

Cécile

A City day. You decide to come back to the Mountains earlier by yourself. I am haunted by visions of you doing something terrible to yourself. I have hidden belts and horse leads, but who knows. Your fate is in your damaged hands. I have to relearn to trust you as you regain your independence.

I cannot wait till I see the back of my last client and can drive home. I am never sure whether I will find you alive. Sometimes I am so frightened of finding you hanging from the mezzanine rail.

I try to accept that it is your life, which means you might choose to kill yourself. But I cannot accept that.

Sunday 24 November 2002

Oceane

In our conversations, Cécile seems to ask me more about why I didn't tell her what happened earlier with Seth than about what actually happened.

On one level, there is no good reason why I didn't tell her. It is not that I didn't trust her, or that I thought she wouldn't believe me. It is just how our relationship has always been, and I knew that telling her about this would make her more sad, worried, maybe even a little guilty.

My first memory, ever, is in France; I would have been nearly three years old and we were at my grandmère's huge summer residence. I have a few memories of this place, but the one I'm thinking of is where I can't find Cécile. I wander down a forest path and then see her from a distance, sitting and looking over the 500-year-old man-made lake, called *l'etang* in that part of France. The striking thing in this memory is the feeling that Cécile was sad. I remember hesitating, somehow knowing something was wrong. I remember seeing her thin hunched shoulders as she held her arms around her knees, and I can still remember the feeling that I shouldn't interrupt. That she was fragile. There is a part of me that has never stopped seeing her that way.

A few years later, when I was five or six, she told me of her history of rape, as a five-year-old and then the gang rape she endured as a young adult.

So I never wanted to tell Cécile about Seth in case she saw it as a failure on her part to stop this from happening in the next generation. A small part of me also feels that what happened to me is insignificant compared to what she experienced – it feeds my shame. One of my lifelong recurring beliefs is that I am making a bigger deal than I should about a situation. The little voice in my head always tells me: 'You are making such a fuss over nothing. People experience far worse things every day – what have you really got to complain about?'

But I also don't tell Cécile that my silence isn't only to do with her; it is as much about my own shame. My doubt about whether I'd been 'asking for it'. As the dean pointed out to me with such delight when I told him, I was displaying some 'strange behaviours' at the time. I didn't lock my door after the first time Seth came into my room and tried to force himself on me. I didn't say anything to anyone else until the third time. I didn't tell him to get out of my room when I felt uncomfortable with him there, even before any of it happened.

The reasons for my silence are many. It goes back to memories of not having my boundaries respected. To feeling like I had to laugh at jokes or comments about my breasts or changing body in adolescence. And it goes back to much earlier years, of memories that cause shame and discomfort. These memories may be fuzzy but they have stayed in my body and made the sexual assault at college feel too much like a repetition. But I think I needed my independence, and running back to your mother does not help with that.

Another potential reason: did part of me want to punish Cécile for not protecting me when I was younger? Cécile, maybe part of me feels that you had your chance and failed, and this time with Seth I didn't trust you enough to give you even a chance to protect me. So I retreat into my shell. I know you are troubled and curious, but there is too much history – so much left unsaid and not dealt with in the past. It's not that I want you to suffer or to be left wondering exactly what happened in my childhood, but there are too many emotions at stake. Seeing you were not there for me then, why should I go through the embarrassment and shame of dredging it up again now that I'm feeling vulnerable?

Cécile

The house is still quiet. As usual I come and lie down next to you, enjoying the sweet smell that emanates from your body after a night's sleep. I do not remember how the conversation starts. I am not sure why I ask you whether the college looked after you properly, protected you. I tell you I have had this image in my head for a while of a boy coming into your room in the middle of the night and trying to rape you. Then you tell me how that did happen. You tell me of the gagging so you could not scream. Three times, it happened.

'Did he actually rape you?'

'No, he didn't.'

You had to fight seriously, though. Once you grabbed a pen from your desk and stabbed his hand and it bled. A huge weight comes over me – the weight of the sexual aggressions and violations I myself endured, the aloneness. I so much hoped that you at least would be protected.

'Why didn't you tell me, Oceane?'

If only you had told me maybe you wouldn't have needed to go through the terrors, depression and suicide.

'Why didn't you let me help?'

How I used to wish I had a mother I could have talked to of the dirty hands in packed metros probing my twelve-year-old undeveloped genitals, of the flashers in the park, of the strange men following me in the street when I went to visit my sister Odile in Paris. In our family these were taboo areas and there was no warning of the dangers awaiting little girls in the world. Besides, my visits to Odile at that time were secret. I was not supposed to travel through Paris on my own, but Odile had been thrown out by our father, who was furious at her determination to study medicine – 'girls become nurses, not doctors'. I was her only contact with the family.

'I did not want to upset you. I knew it would upset you.'

The extremes children go to in order to protect their parents. Are they not more upsetting?

'Were you worried how I would react?'

'Not really. Just that ignorance is bliss.'

That leaves me diminished. I have no desire to be ignorant.

Later, in our weekly sessions, my therapist Isabella will remark on the silence. The silence between my mother and me. Even now, not telling my mother what I am going through with my own child. The silence between that child and me.

'Oceane wants to know about you, like you so much wanted to know about your mother,' she says.

Earlier this year, Oceane, you actually started to tell me about your silent self. You explained the role you had taken as a child, looking after me. About how, after all the shouting and anger, you would find me in the shower with tears pouring down my face, and you could not say anything.

In such chaos and violence, there had been no space for you to have a voice, to speak up, to scream. I failed to recognise your distress; I failed to help you out of your silence. I am sorry, Oceane, I am so sorry. Your quiet, gentle nature gave me comfort. I knew that what was happening at home was not good for you; at times I wondered how it would come out later, but I never thought you might turn against your own self. Oceane, I hope you can find your way out of the silence. I have relished the moments in the recent past when you have broken through. Your speaking is so welcome.

Monday 25 November 2002

Cécile

You hear me pottering in the kitchen and call out: 'Mumsk! Can you come in?'

'Coming!'

'Can you help me find a solicitor?'

'You want a solicitor?'

'Yes, I just want to find out about my rights.'

'That's a good idea. There is a women's legal centre in the City. I have heard very good things about them. Would you like me to look it up?'

'Yes, please, could you do that?'

I recognise the determined, stubborn Oceane who is not afraid to be different. The Oceane who – five years old – came to me as I was doing the evening washing-up at the sink: 'Cécile, I want to go to normal school. I do not want to stay at the Steiner school.' And me just taking a breath under the guise of drying my hands, knowing there was more to come. 'I want to learn to read and write now. They just play in my class. I want to read and write.'

Or the Oceane who – nine years old and by now a fluent reader – points at an advertisement for a sign-language course in an adult education brochure left on the kitchen table and announces: 'This is what I want to learn!' And secures herself a place in the course meant for adults.

After I have tracked the legal centre's number and checked that they still exist, you lock yourself in your room with the phone.

When you come out I ask: 'You want to do something about this boy?'

'Yes, that and other things,' you say in a tone that tells me not to ask more.

My heart races. What are the 'other things'? Later as we are sitting on the veranda, warming our skins in the sun, I ask you if you can tell me.

'No, it is my business.'

I'm left terrified.

Oceane

I have been fuming since the awful conversation at college when they kicked me out. Likewise since my room was packed into boxes, my privacy invaded. In my post-suicidal high, I have rediscovered some of my usual oomph – my fighting spirit. I will call lawyers. I will not let them get away with this behaviour. And I will not let them treat anyone else like they did me. I have a glimpse of future purpose and strength, and something warm and positive is kindled inside me. Maybe this can be my purpose. A lifeline.

I ask Cécile for ideas, and she suggests a legal centre in the City that specialises in supporting women. I can see her curiosity – she asks me whether this is about taking action against Seth.

For some reason that is a secondary priority. With him, I have a strange sense that what happened, happened. My overarching feeling is that it was how everything was handled by the college that led to my downward spiral rather than the actual events themselves. I think I could have survived the assaults if I hadn't been made to feel so ashamed by it all – and if I hadn't been intimidated and re-traumatised for nine months afterwards.

If I had to prioritise what I want resolved when it comes to college, I think it would go something like:

Mishandling of the assault (not suggesting that I go to the police, not allowing me to be questioned by a female, not referring me to counselling or giving me resources, even going behind my back and speaking to Seth).

Kicking me out without warning me.

Packing up my room without telling me.

Breaching my privacy by telling so many students at college what I did.

Writing it down crystallises my purpose, although my tummy is alive with butterflies.

I ring the number for the women's legal resource centre and speak to a kind-sounding lady. I start off all jumbled with my words – apologetic for interrupting her day, saying, 'I'm not sure if this is something you can help me with.' But then it becomes smoother – I pick up momentum and remind myself of what I am most aggrieved about. I get to the end of the story – skimming over the details of the assault by Seth at the start of my year at college, the meeting with the dean about it, the decline in my mental health, and then my attempt and the reaction by the college.

The woman on the phone is quiet for a moment and then says, 'I would really like to make sure that we can help you.' She tells me she will speak to her supervisor and get back to me.

Hanging up the phone, a little rush of adrenalin runs through me.

An hour later, the woman calls back. She is suggesting that my case be referred to one of the top law firms in the City. The women's legal resource centre, she explains, has relationships with firms that offer a certain amount of pro bono advice and assistance as part of their warm-fuzzy-feel-good initiatives. She asks me if that is OK, and when I say yes, tells me that someone from the firm will be in touch soon.

Phew! I am tingly with anticipation. It feels so good to be fighting back. Some of the old Oceane is back after lying beaten and dormant for so long. It feels fucking awesome.

Letter from college master

Dear Cécile,

It was good to spend a little time with you when you popped in with Oceane a couple of weeks back. I hope that in our conversation I managed to communicate that I feel the College is not staffed with the expertise to manage the trials currently faced by Oceane. It is a good and kind community at its best, and I hope that Oceane has found genuine friendship and some happiness while she has been here. It was certainly our privilege to have a student so intelligent and delightful in her own unique way. Perhaps you do not know, but she was nominated as 'Citizen of the Year' by one student who clearly believed that Oceane was the most significant person in College for her (or him?).

But it would be unkind to her and unfair to her peers and tutors to allow her to come back to College next year, for we could not give her the guarantees that she now needs that we could care for her responsibly. I have raised this matter with the College Board. They agree with me, and we know that you will accept our decision as you make arrangements for Oceane, medically and residentially, for the year ahead.

Yours sincerely.

Tuesday 26 November 2002

Cécile

Another drive to the City. I am taken back to a weekend afternoon last winter. We were quietly sitting in the lounge, when you suddenly asked me something about your childhood. That day I explained to you I was worried because you did not know how to protect yourself, how to push away. It took me so many years to learn that for myself.

After listening attentively you said: 'Oh ... so you cared about me.'

Oh God! Didn't you know?

Today though, all these months later, I consider your question in a different light. I want to ask you what you really meant.

I am scared of pushing you over the edge, Oceanette. Either choice – asking you or staying silent – could be detrimental to you. The thread of hope you are holding on to is so tenuous and could be broken so easily.

I take the risk and ask you.

You stare at the road ahead.

'I do not want to answer.'

So I am kept not knowing. If there is nothing more to this, why don't you just reassure me? And if there is, could you be furious at my past blind denial or naivety?

We drive on silently.

It is lunchtime as you walk out of the hand clinic, casts off, your wounds hardly concealed by a patch of sticky bandage, your frozen left hand unprotected. I feel scared for you. We both agree that you need proper bandages and slings before facing the world. Your fragility needs to be made visible.

Later, when I drop you off at uni, with your two bright white slings in place, one of your friends, who has been watching for your arrival, jumps in joy at the sight of you. Later still, you send me an SMS: 'Having such a good time!' Your connection with your friends brings hope to my heart.

Oceane

Early start today. I am only just beginning to feel like I've gotten rid of the anaesthetic in my body. Sometimes in the morning I still wake up with that sense that I've been in a coma-like sleep. I am used to vivid, wild dreams that stay with me when I wake, but for the last month I have woken with complete blankness in my mind. I keep this feeling of blankness for the whole car trip. I won't answer the question Cécile asked me this morning – for the same reason I couldn't talk to her about Seth. Too little too late. I still don't know if I don't want to give Cécile the answer or if I simply cannot.

My weekly visit at the hospital thankfully distracts me. The doctor tells me that he will remove my casts. I am suddenly panicked. But before I can ask any questions, I am whisked down into the dungeon of the hospital. We literally go underground and through a myriad corridors all the way to the 'plaster room'.

Here there are kids (and one or two adults) waiting to have casts put on or removed from their arms or legs. When I was in primary school, I used to dream of the thrill of having a broken arm – I was always envious of those kids with the bright white casts, soon covered with autographs, doodles, comments, wishes. Now I have two still-pristine casts of my own; I am too old for the traditional graffiti-ing.

All of a sudden, the casts are off. I don't know how to hold my arms; they stick out stiffly from my sides. They are covered in old brown iodine stains and I can see the rows and rows and rows of minuscule black stitches. My wrists are like little twigs; it wouldn't take much to snap them. The skin that is not stained is dead white.

My arms are not ready for this. I can't cope with them being exposed. Every slight movement is torturously painful. I can feel the nerves and tendons screeching in shock. Even things that were easy when I had the casts on (wriggling my fingers or picking something up) suddenly feel impossible.

The doctor talks to me about exercises and the importance of using my hands and keeping them clean and a whole lot of other instructions. I am not listening though – I am just wide-eyed panicked about my tender hands being in the big world, unprotected.

Somehow I make it back to the car, where Cécile is waiting. I need to feel like I am independent, and don't like her coming to these appointments. Cécile is shocked when she sees my naked arms. I explain that they have removed the casts because they need to take the stitches out in a few days, and they want me to start using my wrists.

Cécile seems to catch on that I am not OK with this. We go straight to a chemist and pick up arm slings, bandages and elasticised tubing that fits snugly over my wrists and puts a protective layer between me and the world.

With that on, I can finally breathe out. By the time I arrive at uni to see my friends I am no longer holding my arms stiffly by my side.

Wednesday 27 November 2002

Cécile

Today we are again sitting next to each other, looking ahead at the segment of almost-empty highway lit by the headlights, the darkness limiting other visual distractions. The soft drone of the engine at 110 often seems to ease our conversations. In the silences we crank up the Simon and Garfunkel and sing at full voice the old tracks we both love.

We have spent the day in the Capital, visiting Oma and Grandpa – Miranda's parents – who adore you like their own grandchild. You seem exhausted, maybe from your efforts at wearing your joyful front all day, trying to look like you were fully there. You are still hiding, even from those who love you so dearly, maybe even from yourself. I am caught in the guessing game of trying to know what is going on inside your mind, and you are exhausting yourself carrying your load alone.

As we drive, we talk about friends, and loneliness. I tell you how I always considered you one of the most loved people I know.

'Yes,' you reply, 'but when I was in crisis, there was nobody. Nobody wanted to see, to know.'

You say you cannot believe how people did not respond to your obvious calls for help.

'Give me an example,' I say.

'Like I told people I could not face life anymore, that I hated myself.'

'Oceanette, you know, many people say that, not really meaning it. The trouble is you meant it literally.'

Do you believe that people are interested in you only when you feel good or pretend to? I wonder whether you inhabit a world in which others are supposed to know, to guess, although you keep them at bay. You tell me how you cannot come out of yourself, how you need people to come to you. You say that the only people you know love you genuinely are myself, and Oma and Grandpa – 'in their own funny way'.

You wrote some goodbye notes. One to me, you say. So maybe, right to the end you knew that I loved you, that your suicide would hurt me terribly. But then why didn't you call on me when you knew I was worried about you?

True, I have been part of your suffering. Also because you are eighteen, you explain, you are trying to make your own way in the world; having only your mother to go to would be like going backwards instead of moving ahead. I understand, but you could not see a life ahead at the time. I wish you could have gone back to your mum as a temporary withdrawal, to a place of care and protection. The world must have felt so awful and terrifying to you.

Oceanette, did you ever wish I had intervened more? I never know whether to push towards you or respect the distance you seem to need, scared that if I push a bit too insistently, you will withdraw even further. Many times I hear myself probing and sense you tensing up and going into a silence.

You confirm that, yes, if I had pushed you, and come and seen you at college, you would have pushed me away even more strongly. What would you have needed? I ask.

'For you to call Annemaree to talk to me. With her, I would have talked.'

Even looking back, it is not something I would have done easily. You would have probably felt as if I was interfering with your life, that I had gone behind your back or that Annemaree was calling only because she had been asked, not out of genuine concern. And yet you say that it would probably have saved you, and I did not even think of it.

I recognise so much of myself in you, parts I had hoped you would be spared.

Since you tried killing yourself, you have made an effort to stop calling me that distancing 'Mother', which I never liked. When not the usual 'Cécile', I have become Mama, Maman or even the funny Mumsk.

Oceane, I understand you need people to come to you, but you also need to reach out and feel that when you do, there will be people there for you. Your demand for privacy has alienated the few of my own friends that you have agreed I can talk to. Their silence and tiptoeing around you is uncomfortable, frustrating, anxiety-creating.

As you had feared, you say, your experience right now is of people withdrawing at great speed. 'It's like they all rushed in while I was in hospital and now they have bounced back. I don't know how far away they are going to run.' I wonder if you are lost in self-doubt and see people withdrawing when in fact they are probably trying to respect your demand for privacy.

'Are you sure it's not because it is nearly Christmas time? People do become more occupied with their families. And that you have not let people come really close?'

I think of Miranda, who hasn't been around for a while although she is supposedly your other mother, the good one. Is she one who has bounced back? Do you feel let down by her?

I remember Odile's suicide note, how she wrote her death would soon be just a discreet little news item in the local paper, which was probably right but did not preclude the devastation it would cause for those who did love her, or to whom she was connected even though invisibly.

Oceane

Having my casts off means that I can finally wash on my own. I enjoy having my privacy back, but still find myself calling Cécile in to give my back a good scrub. There is something nice about starting the day with the feeling of being scrubbed clean.

Today we hit the road for the Capital. I am excited about seeing Oma and Grandpa, but I can't help thinking about what they will say and how awkward it might be.

I plan to stick to safe topics – the fact that I finished my exams, what has changed in their house and garden since I last visited.

Oma and Grandpa were a little safe haven for me during my time in the Capital. Since Miranda and Oliver separated earlier this year they technically aren't even my 'step-grandparents' anymore. But they welcomed me into their family with their beautiful big hearts and have made sure I know that no matter what Miranda and Oliver do, they are in my life for good. They feel like my real grandparents – they are the only grandparents I've really had in my life. When I moved to the Capital they would have me for dinner once a week (cooking my favourite meal, of course), let me do a load of washing, and send me home with leftovers for lunch. I think it was one of the reasons Cécile and Oliver agreed to me moving there so young, knowing that they would help me if I was ever in trouble.

One memory sticks with me: Oma, in her husky smoker's voice, saying, 'You have to make sure to see something beautiful every day. It doesn't matter if it is a leaf that is a beautiful colour, or a momentary flash of sunlight at a beautiful angle, just see something beautiful every day.' I think she must have said that to me every time I visited, and I've never tired of it.

Thursday 28 November 2002

Cécile

Today you confide that you are starting to have some glimpse of a different life for yourself. You seem to have no illusion about your destructive side and to accept the fact that it will need attention over a long time.

I have arranged to meet a friend for coffee. I tell her about starting to write diary notes to help myself with the trauma of the last weeks. I tell her how it is coming out in the form of a letter to you. She straightens her back; her face stiffens as she stares at me.

'Are you going to give it to her?'

'Of course not. This is for myself, it is very personal. It's just that I find myself talking to her in my mind a lot, you know. I am just writing it down.'

Her voice takes on a magisterial tone. 'There is a problem about boundaries,' she announces. 'I have been very concerned about your dream, about you telling Oceane about it. I think it might have influenced what she did. I think it pushed her to suicide.'

The dream rushes back to me: We are walking in a

town along a bridge, Oceane. We are happy, we laugh. Then we bump into a woman who is holding a baby. She asks us if we would mind holding her baby while she goes to the toilet in the basement under the bridge. Of course not; we both love babies and like to help. As she disappears downstairs, I wonder to myself if you have had trouble with some depraved man in that public toilet. Just as I think that, you run to the rail guard, jump off to what I know is concrete underneath. I run to the stairs and wake up before knowing whether you are alive.

My friend is telling me I nearly killed you with this dream. I try to remind her how I had agonised over it. It's not as if I had thoughtlessly rushed to tell you of it. I only told you after months and months of pondering over what it meant, over what to do with it.

I remind her of my alarm at the sense that something was going terribly wrong with you that you were not letting me know about. You kept telling me you were OK and yet you were not sleeping, very stressed, very angry, not eating properly. You were not responding to my messages of concern and nobody seemed to hear my alarm. All the friends I shared my dream with seemed to dismiss my concern. 'Stop worrying, go to bed,' a friend had said one night.

But you were not OK, Oceane. One day over the phone, it must have been days before you tried to kill yourself, you tentatively let me know that you were nauseous all the time. 'You are not pregnant?' I asked, half wishing you might have frolicked around with some boy. 'No,' you said, and went on to confide that you had been put on antidepressants.

'What happened?'

'I broke down.'

You would not explain much except that you had collapsed and community mental health had been called in. Their psychiatrist had prescribed an antidepressant.

After a few days of you getting worse, hating the side effects of the antidepressant and yet being told to increase the dose, I decided to demonstrate the extent of my concern for you by sharing the dream.

'Oceane, I am worried because I have had this dream about you a while back and I can't work out whether it is about you or about me. Would it be OK if I told you the dream, and you can just tell me if it resonates with you, just that?'

I tell you my dream, reliving the awful feeling.

'Does it resonate, Oceane?'

'Yes,' you say with no hesitation. 'But I can't tell you more.'

And then Oceane, a few days later, I did nearly lose you. And now my friend is saying that it was me who nearly killed you.

'It was *your* dream,' she tells me. 'I think it was about your own suicidality.'

She sounds so sure of herself, a caricature of the traditional interpretative analyst.

'It is about something running in your family that has not been resolved.'

I am not suicidal and have not been for many, many years. Not that there has not been a lot of suicidality in my family. I have spent years of therapy working at that. Just as I also spent months looking at that dream from all angles.

Recently, Oceane, I asked you about how you felt about me telling you the dream.

'It upset me.' But again you cannot tell me more.

I would so much like to know how and when suicide became an option for you. I know that life didn't start easy for you, and it only became harder and harder as time went on. I know you felt that you had to do life on your own. Did it bother you to realise that however hard you had wanted to protect me I had some understanding of what was going on?

This morning you tell me how it is important not to keep self-sacrificing. Important to let yourself have some of the things that make you feel good: nice clothes, for example, are important. We decide to throw away all the old ones you do not really like and splurge – a bit.

Saturday 30 November 2002

Cécile

Today is one of those days when it just all feels too hard, Oceane. I feel stretched to my limits, emotionally, financially. I find myself constantly on the verge of the very tears that you said used to upset you so much when you were little. Now I am acutely aware of these tears, how they overwhelm you, how they have been part of what has killed you inside. So I fight to keep them in. It makes my friends think that I am not emotional. They do not understand that my pain, if I let it show, endangers you.

I still do not know what is going on inside that little head of yours. So difficult to read you beyond the 'I am fine' you throw back at my questions. 'I want to do it all alone,' you add.

Saturday 7 December 2002

Oceane

An ordinary day in so many ways but for one significant moment. A friend of Cécile's came to visit. She took me aside, out to the veranda, and said how sorry she was to hear of what I had done, and the pain I must have been in. It was very sincere, short and to the point, and she had tears coming down her face.

Her words and her tears are well and truly embedded in my mind. It was a very raw exposure to how people would have felt if I had succeeded in killing myself. More powerful as it was someone I don't know well and would not have expected to care. So many people ignore what I have done, even when I know they know. I say I prefer it that way. But I realise seeing this person's reaction that the silence of other people is painful. This reaction felt kind of good. A moment when the pain on the inside is matched with the pain on the outside of someone else.

Sunday 8 December 2002

Oceane

Another car trip, another conversation. Cécile and I revisit my childhood. She seems to be intent on understanding my memories of it. So many places she has a complete blank and I am left scrabbling to fill in entire events with my childish perspective on them. It makes it feel a bit like these things didn't happen, or that they were not important enough to recall. My entire childhood is built on these painful memories and Cécile can barely remember them. Occasionally she just says, 'Oh yes, I do remember that,' as if I was talking about an old favourite toy that got lost or something trivial. It's not trivial to me, Cécile – cruel jokes, black eyes, screaming death threats, my sense of safety constantly shattered.

Cécile asks me more questions, and I tell her the deep secret that has lurked in the back of my mind for years. 'I wish I had been fostered out or adopted.'

The first time I had this thought was after playing at a friend's house. We'd spent a blissful afternoon playing make-believe games and their parents had dropped me home. I remember arriving home and feeling the tense, brewing thunderstorm of anger thick in the air. Who knows what it was about. I thought I could avoid it, stay in my little happy bubble, but then it all exploded in typical fashion, and as I looked at the broken furniture and glass, I thought, 'I wish my friend's parents could have seen this and taken me back home with them.'

Then, one day when I was twelve, the boys and I were at Oliver's, not long after the separation. I can't remember how it started, but an enormous fight broke out over dinner, and Oliver snapped and called the police. The police came and, seeing the mess, called a social worker from Child Welfare. I remember her coming a few times and chatting to my brothers. Despite the fact that I had been there when everything happened, she never asked to speak to me. For months I hoped that the social worker would notice me and that maybe I'd get a foster family. I'm not sure I ever quite recovered from that sense of invisibility or unimportance.

I can sense Cécile's hurt at hearing this, but I feel lighter from having finally aired something I have kept hidden for so many years. It is not that this has anything to do with my suicidality; it is just that I want Cécile to understand how difficult and painful I found so much of my childhood.

I remember Cécile taking me, age eight maybe, to go house hunting ('we're leaving the boys'). We looked at a property with a little grassy backyard and a big bending tree that I knew would be great for climbing. We returned home a few hours later and never mentioned the escape to anyone. But for the following days, weeks, months and even years, I would daydream about how much better life could have been if we had gone through with the plan to start afresh in that safe little house with the good climbing tree.

Agenda for meeting with college dean and master

As requested, brief of the points I wish to discuss on our arranged meeting (9th December 02).

I would like to address my concerns over some of the decisions made by you following recent events. In particular:

My personal belongings were packed without any attempt to gain permission from me, or even informing me after it had been done. This was a breach of my privacy, and also resulted in some of my possessions missing (3 CDs, a new watch, earrings), and damaged photos.

I seem to have been dismissed from College and banned from the grounds till the end of semester without formal notice or any communication.

Other students on my wing were informed of what happened without my permission or knowledge of it, I experience this as another breach of privacy, that has caused me a lot of distress.

I would also like to discuss the handling of the events in March 02, concerning Seth Thornton. This has raised questions about your duty of care for me:

Contents of report written by the College.

Insufficient personal support or offer of professional help (recognition of the impact of the incidents reported on my mental and emotional state).

Inadequate follow-up to ensure that I felt the problems had been resolved and that I felt safe in College.

I appreciate your willingness to discuss my concerns, and I hope we can work towards a better resolution.

Regards,

Oceane

Monday 9 December 2002

Oceane

Today was the big college meeting. After Cécile received that infuriating letter from the master I decided to set up an attempt at conciliation before proceeding with the lawyers. I didn't know what to expect from it, but I was fired up for the chance to tell them what is on my mind.

I tossed and turned all night, thinking it through. Practising what I wanted to say, imagining what they might say. In my head, the scenario swung wildly from boring, mundane conversations, to the master and dean becoming enraged and striking out at me to shut me up. I pictured apologies on their part, promises to repay the six weeks of rent owed to me. I rehearsed passionate arguments in my mind – by the time morning finally came I felt ready to give Martin Luther King Jr a run for his money.

Annemaree came with me – I just didn't feel like I could face those two on my own. I love how articulate and strong she is, and I was so relieved she was there.

I felt sick to my stomach during the hour-and-a-half drive up, but at least the trip passed quickly as we planned how we want the meeting to go and I filled Annemaree in on the details of what has happened with the college. It helped me to tell her, partly because it was another way of practising what I want to say, and partly because it also sparked up my fighting spirit.

The conversation I had with the women's legal resource centre had given me confidence. Now I just needed to find the right balance between certainty based on positive, healing energy and the righteousness of a spoilt, dummy-spitting Gen-Y. I needed a pinch of righteousness to pick myself up and out of suicidal ideation, but not so much that I become a bully in retaliation.

The meeting went for two hours. We wrapped things up quickly at the end – Annemaree could see we weren't getting anywhere. In some ways I was disappointed to leave it; I was getting into my arguments and picking apart their excuses. Annemaree was right though: it was turning into 'he said, she said' and we probably could have argued all day.

The dean and the master obviously thought Annemaree was some weird hippie crazy lady – but it was great that they couldn't put anything over her. So many times during the meeting I thought, 'Thank God she is here!' Not only as a witness to all that was being said, but also because of her clarity and the sharpness and intelligence of her responses.

The dean in particular was in bullying mode throughout the whole meeting. The master has a calmer, more controlled personality, but is cold and hard as cement underneath. He had to pull the dean back a few times when he started getting too openly aggressive – although he wasn't able to prevent him making one appalling comment at the end of the meeting.

We had been talking about how the college had responded to my allegations against Seth – how they had not offered counselling or suggested going to the police. They said that they were just respecting my wish that no one else know about it.

Annemaree said that when a young woman undergoes a trauma, she might be scared and need privacy but that doesn't mean you can't bring in support for her. She said maybe they needed to use more imagination.

Anyway, the dean said something about me not expressing clearly enough what I wanted, and that it reminded him of a case in South Australia where a judge had said publicly that sometimes when females say no, they really mean yes. The dean actually had the gall to say that perhaps it wasn't fair that the judge got in trouble in the media for his comment, because it seemed that sometimes females are confused about what they want (like me, he added) and when females say no, it is clear that sometimes they do mean yes. He actually said that!

While he didn't make the comment in relation to the actual assault, it was like he thought he could get away with saying it in the context of whether or not to respect my expressed wish for privacy.

In a way it was satisfying to hear the dean say this: I knew even when I first had to tell him about what had happened that he was judging me and that he believed that I'd asked for it somehow. It was almost a relief to hear him say it out loud.

The rest of the meeting was less eventful. They smarmed, smirked, debated their way out of everything. Why did they pack up my room? Oh, because the doctors told them I'd be unlikely to survive. And it was for my own good – they were just worried about my safety and my needs. Why did they tell people at college? Oh, they had a duty of care to all the students, and it was important to be open and supportive of them.

One point they delighted in expressing was that when I took the action I did (to attempt suicide), I lost my human rights and therefore had no right to my place at college. It was such a strange argument, I found it hard not to laugh. They used the analogy (in case I was too stupid to understand them the first time) that if an illegal refugee was found to be living at college, they would have a duty to evict that person and give them to the police, and then pack up their room. Leaving aside the rights of refugees (which was hard, believe me!) – suicide is not a crime.

When we got out, I gulped in the sunshine and fresh air gratefully. I felt so energised that I could have run a marathon. Instead, we headed to the outer City for some Lebanese food, using most of the half-hour drive there to debrief.

Then, over lunch, Annemaree suddenly asked me straight up about my earlier memories. We were sitting side by side at this stage, in a little cafe booth, with Turkish bread and dips to snack on. She just came out and asked me directly.

I said I had been touched inappropriately, and then I had to focus on the food because I was trying not to cry.

In some ways it was a relief to have someone ask – because no one ever had, not even the various child welfare agency workers or teachers who had commented on my sadness or regular absence from school. But I was also completely unprepared and had no idea how to respond. It was the first time I had said anything to anyone about it, and the look in Annemaree's eyes made me want to cry: I saw genuine sadness, deep caring, worry, and a tinge of disappointment with the world.

I think Annemaree could see I was struggling and we dropped it, without saying anything further.

Inside, I felt a strange rush of elation mixed with fearful anticipation. I was also conscious that my words could be ambiguous.

In a black-and-white world, 'inappropriate touching' implies sexual abuse. But that was not exactly what I meant. I need words in between – that tell of my discomfort and sense that my body was never completely mine. I need words that describe not feeling completely safe or respected in my bodily autonomy. I need words that say how much it impacted on my sense of control and consent. It left me with the twisted belief that I didn't get to have a final say about what was OK or not OK for me. And that had a disastrous outcome so many years later.

Why didn't I lock the door to Seth? Why didn't I do more to protect myself? Why wasn't I sure about what I wanted or didn't want?

Was I overreacting?

What I did know was that I couldn't bear another sexual joke. Or pinch or squeeze. I couldn't bear another comment on my 'shapely body' or my 'pert breasts'. But I couldn't find those words, and my response to Annemaree felt both freeing and misleading.

Friday 13 December 2002

Oceane

The mornings are always my favourite – it seems everything is softer in the morning. Cécile is less tense, less likely to bring up serious conversations before breakfast. We can potter around each other, making big pots of black tea for her, and grinding coffee beans for me in the familiar wooden French moulin. Breakfast chatter flows easily. Cécile often asks me about my dreams but I haven't started dreaming again since my attempt. My nights are still blank spaces, like the hours have just been snipped out of my life's film reel.

I'm a bit on edge this morning as I have a meeting with the law firm that I've been set up with. When I need cheering up, I have been googling the firm and looking at all their awards and accolades and successes. The lawyers in the photos are professional, corporate, sharp. Two minutes spent on their website, and I feel great.

It's a smooth trip to the City. I don't mind talking to Cécile about the college stuff. I even like talking it through, clarifying in my mind what I want to say –

what I want to focus on. I really want to be clear about the outcome I'm hoping for and the things that are important to me. I'm starting to realise just how much of my happiness I've invested in this path. I need something to mark the moment of choosing life, and have a sense that this might be it. By taking legal action I am proving to myself that I am empowered and efficacious, responsible, and not a victim – all the things that I lost in my experience with Seth and the flow-on effects of the college's actions.

Cécile drops me off and I go up in the elevator. It is one of those huge buildings right in the centre of the City, where there are different elevators for different floors. I stand out like a sore thumb with my homemade green skirt and hippie white singlet. Out of the elevator, the law firm's reception area is amazing. It spans nearly the entire wall of the building, with floor-to-ceiling windows, leather couches everywhere, and impressive statues and other art pieces dotted around the centre of the room in glass casing. All the art is Aboriginal, as are the names of the meeting rooms. It is a good sign. They must be socially conscious and progressive.

The receptionist is friendly and must be used to seeing the pro bono cases walk in, because she doesn't blink an eye, but just tells me to take a seat and offers me a drink while I am waiting. Five minutes later three lawyers walk through the door, and I know it's them a second before they see me. They are sassy, well-dressed young women and I feel a smile bubble up in me.

I can't quite shake hands yet with my arms, which makes for a moment of awkwardness. These women are used to firm handshaking.

We go into a room, and someone comes in to take our drinks order – the lawyers all order coffees but I am too nervous to have anything other than water. They introduce themselves properly – two are more senior lawyers in the firm, and the other is at associate level. I am on one side of a huge long board table, and they are like a panel in front of me. All of them are incredibly beautiful and confident. I feel myself straighten and sit taller in their company.

We spend over an hour talking. I skip over the year quickly, and tell them about the final ten days before I attempted suicide: I tell them of going to the local community mental health centre and the prescription for Zoloft, which at that point was too late – I had more or less made up my mind. I talk of the last weekend, the valedictory dinner and nominations for 'citizen of the year', then of hearing Seth call out to me late on the Sunday night as I was trying to find my keys to get back inside. How the panic started to course through me, and how I was not able to calm myself. I summarise my suicide attempt: the cutting, the pills, the plastic bag, the additional pills, the hanging and the eventual defeat and rush to hospital.

I feel strong, certain in my words, strangely removed from myself as well. Although I've repeated this history to so many doctors in hospital, I am not scared of the details this time. Talking felt dangerous there, with the psychiatrists' judgemental comments and coldness, but here I feel light and strong and proud for surviving. I don't need to omit anything or censor myself. I am also talking about it in the past tense for the first time.

I tell them about the college telling everyone what I'd done, packing up my room, evicting me with no notice or reason. The lawyers write frantically, all three of them taking down every word. I lap up their serious but compassionate expressions. Everything feels crystal clear. Every word spoken, every clink of a cup or glass, the grain of the wood on the table, the blueness of the sky outside.

When I finish talking, I want them to just say, 'Yes, we'll fight your case,' but obviously that is not how the real world works. They tell me they'll discuss the details and be in touch early next week. But I walk out smiling properly, with my whole face and spirit.

To top off what has already been probably my best day in nine months, I go to yoga and have another private lesson. After that, I feel like I could fly. This feeling is worth living for. Yes.

Sunday 15 December 2002

Cécile

Our conversations are gradually becoming easier. They seem to follow a thread.

'I am not angry with you,' you say. But you can't be close to me, you add, because I left you to cope on your own with too much when you were a child.

'You could have done something. You could have arranged for me to live somewhere else. I should have left when I was eleven.'

You did not run away like your brothers did. Your screams stayed locked inside and you remained the trouble-free, quiet child, and it could have killed you.

What makes it worse for you is that I actually had a sense of how bad it was for you and I did nothing to help you.

Sometimes, this just feels like a painfully ironical repetition of my situation with my own mother. A mother I so much desired to be close to, but who was not available. Not out of ill will, just a combination of circumstances and personality. For years I was so angry with her, for not having let me have a mother. And then it was too late; all longing had died off. I have never managed to find a relationship with her.

Now it is you telling me: 'It is too late, I needed you earlier.'

Maybe I am being punished. Oh, Oceanette, I hope we can change history. Please, let me be your mother.

You know, Oceanette, from the time you were only six weeks old till you were just over one, I carried you around everywhere on my hip, in a pouch, everywhere, body to body. We were living in a tent in the outback of Far North Queensland, no pram, no cot, no washing machine, and I could not put you down anywhere, not even on a blanket because the green ants would smell your sweetness and within minutes attack you. Carrying you close, I knew that you were safe while I tended to more than I could: Julian, two and a half years old, his asthma, his insecurity; Leon, only fourteen months, ready to explore the whole world; Oliver, constantly hungry for attention. I carried you everywhere, I felt you, but I did not look at you, did not see you, not then, and not as you grew.

Wednesday 18 December 2002

Cécile

Sometimes it feels that you can only take from me materially. That it is the only way you let me help you. Almost like a revenge. As if, because I could not give you what you needed when you were little, you are taking what you can now.

I feel ashamed at thinking that way.

Isabella says: 'Oceane may be punishing you for not being there. Can you accept the way her anger expresses itself, in her demands, in her sense of entitlement?'

During the night I wake up thinking of your depression as depletion; your asking me to buy so many things for you as an attempt to fill yourself up. You have been starved of mothering.

You say I should have let you be looked after by another family. But wouldn't you have resented that later? I reel inside and my tortured head is full of self-defence pleas.

Oceane, do you remember the afternoon I took you to look for a house to rent? I felt we were trapped in a never-ending cycle. I could not manage it anymore. We would create a home of peace. The places we saw looked dark and shabby and grim, like rented places often do, loveless, care starved. Oliver always pleaded with me not to go, saying that he would make an effort, and I always softened and hoped again.

And then years later, instead of us creating a house of peace, just the two of us, you ended up going to live with Oliver after the final separation. Was it the appeal of Miranda, like a big sister? Being away from the boys and their troubles? But it wasn't so easy in reality. Do you remember how you could not tell Oliver that you were coming to see me? You had to pretend you were walking the dog and you would secretly drop in for a little while.

You know, Oceane, I never abandoned you in all that time, never resented you for your choice although it was so painful to see you living with Oliver. You were on my mind every day.

Wednesday 8 January 2003

Cécile

You get back from the City with your friend Ben, your wrists comfortably naked.

Ben is a good friend – reserved, a little shy, but playful and always polite and caring towards you. I love seeing the easy banter you two have. I am so thrilled when I see you more and more often without bandages or bracelets to camouflage your scars. You have moved a long way towards owning and accepting your wanting to die. You are a courageous young woman.

You are planning your move back to the City for uni. You are so happy tonight at having found the 'perfect house' for the four of you to share. The images of your new life are shaping themselves and as they do your anxiety seems to diminish and your hope becomes more solid. But my anxiety increases: it seems so soon.

Will you create a safety net? Will you reach out? Will we, the ones who care for you, read your signs and find ways to act on them? I realise how, in the lead-up to your attempt, you isolated everyone around you by demanding total confidentiality from each of us separately. The little bits you gave each of us were worrying but nobody had the whole picture of your mental state, and everyone promised to keep the very silence that was killing you, and became trapped in that alienating secrecy. Will you do that again?

Oceane, our concern is going to irritate you; of course you do not want to feel watched over, and yet how not to? So, for your own sake and for our sake, the less anxious we can be, the better. We, your supporters, need to be able to talk to each other, especially if we are worried, or wondering about you. And we need to be able to trust you.

Wednesday 15 January 2003

Cécile

Your depression seems to be creeping back. Your face has closed in and you are keeping me out here in the cold. Reaching out is becoming difficult for each of us. I feel tortured, tormented and empty. Is this the way you too feel inside?

Two am. Once again I wake up in a startle. Keeping the phone next to me allows me a few hours of sleep, but then the anguish takes over. 'Stay present and hold her gently,' I repeat to myself.

Knowing that suicide is still an option for you terrifies me. I am convinced that with time and the right support you can experience life, its joys and pains. If only somebody could reassure me that you will get through in the end, that you will stay alive, and if only I could believe them.

I have no taste for the emerging day.

Friday 17 January 2003

Cécile

Later this afternoon you'll be flying off to have a holiday with your dear mob at the Bay – the rest of Oma and Grandpa's family. We left mid-morning to look for a futon bed for your new shared home. It's all arranged: I'll buy the futon and Oliver will pay for the base. Looks like we have made progress towards cooperating to help you.

We've found a good futon that will require little maintenance and won't compact – more expensive though. With your hands and wrists, there is no way you will be able to turn a standard futon over for a long time. It is taking all the money I have managed to save during the few weeks I went back to work before Christmas, and I haven't worked since then.

I know how much this new home means to you. I know how much you need a room that will nourish you. Your housemates understand too. They've let you have the largest room, sunlit in the mornings and with an ensuite and a walk-in wardrobe. We want you to feel like a queen.

We walk to another shop where you find the base you want. This base too is not the cheapest, but still so little for what it will give you. It has a head, which will help you with sitting up in bed, reading, studying. And it looks good. I am pretty sure that being so clear about what you like and want is part of finding your way out of the darkness.

You walk outside to call Oliver. I can tell it is still tentative and awkward between you – I don't think it has been long since you opened a little connection to him, but even that information you have kept hidden from me. I don't know when you made contact or how you feel about it. You are always very discreet about not talking to him in front of me. You've learnt to keep the two relationships very separate.

From inside the shop, I see you pace, stop, pace. Why is it taking so long?

I distract myself by browsing among sofas, tables and other furniture I have no interest in. And then you come back into the shop, face undone; your whole body has lost its uprightness.

'Oliver does not want to pay for the base anymore.'

'What? It was all arranged, wasn't it?'

'He's changed his mind. He wants me to take an old base he has at his place.'

God, I wish my credit card was not almost full. I hate this money business. I don't have the energy to call Oliver. I can't bear to listen to his explanations.

'Leave it to me, Oceanette. I am going to find a way. I promise. I promise you'll get this base before you come back from the Bay. OK?'

You wipe your tears, trying to make yourself look OK to go back into the street. I sense that you do not want to fuel my animosity towards your dad. So you keep your feelings about him in. Exactly what you've done for years.

Email from Cécile to various friends

Dear so and so,

I wonder if you could help me. You know what I am going through at the moment. Right now I am trying to help Oceane organise the house she is going to share with friends in the City. She needs a room that feels warm and comfortable.

Yesterday we went and bought a great futon. But then, Oliver, who had promised to pay for the base, has just reneged.

Oceane feels so let down. I wish I could just pay for this base, but it is summer and with all the time I have taken off work, my account is dry. I wonder if you would be willing to contribute a little something towards buying this base.

It would mean so much to her to go to sleep in a bed given by all the people who want her happy.

I hope that is not asking too much.

With love,

Cécile

Saturday 18 January 2003

Oceane

How glorious, I've arrived in the Bay. It was a last-minute arrangement, a happy coincidence of cheap flights and managing to assure Cécile I'll be OK. It feels so good to be somewhere different and feeling more independent.

Mieke, Hans and the girls picked me up at the airport last night – it's been six months since I saw them all. The girls have grown, as they do constantly, and are at a gorgeous age. Yarrow is starting kindergarten in a few weeks, and it is so sweet watching her excitement and seeing Tess being the protective older sister explaining the system to her. I never expected to gain a whole family when Miranda married Oliver but I have. It is the biggest gift from their relationship, and even better is that I get to keep my 'blown in by the wind' family despite Miranda and Oliver's separation.

I feel so welcomed and wrapped up in Mieke and Hans's love. It's hard not to feel loved when they both have tears in their eyes at seeing me – alive. They make me feel grown-up and are so open with their affection compared to what I am used to in my family. Mieke especially – she spontaneously hugs me and says 'I love you'. It's funny, but I'm not used to those three little words – in our family we never said it to each other. I've gone my whole life and never been told those words till Mieke.

A few weeks ago, Mieke wrote me a letter. I've kept it in my wallet and read it a hundred times. I love how her words make me feel seen and understood.

She writes about not wanting anyone to hurt me anymore, including myself: my self-harm hasn't been about attention; it has been about showing on the outside all the hurt that no one can see. That goes right to the bone of one of my huge sensitivities at the moment: the fact that I cannot tolerate the thought or actuality of pain but still crave the finality of death sometimes. I just don't want to hurt myself in the process.

There is one line in the letter that I struggle with: 'once you are better again, you will be glad you survived'. So many people have tried to tell me this but I can't imagine or even conceive that one day I will be grateful for having survived, because if I had died, I would never have known what I would have missed out on by living. Every time people say this kind of thing, I think, 'You have absolutely no fucking idea how much pain I was in, do you?'

Letter from Mieke

Dearest Oceane,

It's six thirty a.m. The kids are awake (sleepily awake), the animals fed and watered and it's a good time for me to sit with a cup of tea (hot, sweet, and strong enough to trot a mouse over) and write to you. It looks like it's going to be a lovely day: the mist is rising from the paddocks, the currawongs are warbling away cheerfully and the kookaburras are laughing. Well, at least people interpret the birdsong as cheerful laughter – but in reality the birds are saying 'rack off ya piece of moving guano, this is my patch' … or something of the like. It's a question of interpretation: we read the signals wrong. Just 'cos the birds sound chirpy, we think they are chirpy. I guess I have been making the same mistake with you – because everything you do, you do so well, and you sound generally cheerful, I didn't think to stop and take stock and find out how you really are doing, inside.

I don't know what happened to start this downwards spiral of lost hope, but whatever (or whoever) it was, I wish I could do something about it. I feel fiercely protective of you right now and I so much wish I could keep you from further harm. I wish I could open some existential window on life and let you feel how nice the breeze is and how gentle the sun can be as it caresses your skin.

And, I want a world with Oceane in it. It's a better and nicer place with you in it. I don't want anyone to hurt you anymore, not even yourself. Just hang in there, Oceane. I realise you must be in terrible pain (I'm not talking about physical pain, though that must be considerable), but once you are better again (and that WILL happen) you will be glad you survived. Your life is precious – it's precious to us, and in time again you will see that it's precious to yourself too. Hang in there, and look for things to hope for, even if they are small things. You are suicidal now, but you will get better, one step at a time. There is so much I want to do with you – small things and large things: I want to go for a swim with you again at that remote cove out on the nature reserve, for one. I want Tess and Yarrow to be able to visit you, and you can show them where you live. I want to go galloping over the beach with you on a pair of good horses. I want to hear what you have to say about life, and how you experience love, and to hear about books you have read.

Your life matters to me, love.

All my love, Mieke

Monday 20 January 2003

Oceane

I feel so nourished after a few days here, spending time with Tess and Yarrow. It is hard not to feel good when you have two little kids doting on you.

Mieke and Hans had a chat to me this evening, asking if I would be the godmother of the girls – in terms of caring for them if anything ever happened to Mieke and Hans. Pretty huge honour and responsibility. I got very choked up when they asked, but I said yes straight away, and we talked about it until pretty late. Perhaps they asked to give me a reason to live, but I don't mind – I've never felt so at home and like I belong as I do with this family.

Despite the conversation with Mieke and Hans, I feel as if I have two switches in my brain.

One says 'LIVE'. *Look at how these people love you; think about what it would be like for them if you died. Life is actually pretty good: remember that walk on the beach and that swim in the waves? There are so many beautiful moments in life if you stop and see them, like Oma says.*

The other switch says 'DIE'. *Think of everything that could go wrong in the future, all the hardships you might have to face, the potential for failure, humiliation, embarrassment, pain, hurt, distress. What if the court case goes wrong and you end up being mocked by the college and the world? What if you have to pay their legal costs? You couldn't live with that.*

So even though now I am in bed, feeling warm and loved, with salty hair from a beautiful day at the beach, I am researching to find a peaceful way to exit this life.

I feel like a traitor thinking of suicide still, having just committed to caring for the girls if something happens to Mieke and Hans. I am trying to use that thought to climb out of this little sinkhole I have fallen into just now.

Cécile, you've been texting me all day. I just can't reply. This is my safe space up here. I know you have proven yourself to me the last few months but there are deep wounds and entrenched habits keeping this chasm between us. I can't force it closed.

Thursday 23 January 2003

Cécile

Your father called today to say he had important information about you.

'She is very suicidal. She told Mieke that she does not feel she is going to make it through the year.'

My heart sinks. This is not news to me but having it thrown in my face only aggravates my fear.

'I know.'

'The Mountains is not "home" for her.'

Thank you. Don't you think I know it is not the perfect place for her? Don't you think I know how hard it's been? Yet is there a better place for her at the moment? The City is too busy. The country, too quiet. At least she is actually in her own home and we are doing what we can day by day. So you can keep your unhelpful comments to yourself.

'I am going to find a home where there is a room for her.'

So you want to take her from me again, to play hero? I am devastated.

'We need to appear as if we get on together, as friends.'

Sorry, I cannot appear. This is real. I am real. You have asked for 'let's pretend we are friends' before – while breaking my trust.

Of course, I know you need both of us there together for you, not fighting. I am not fighting; I have no will or energy for that, but I cannot pretend to be friends. Sometimes, I wonder how your father and I ever got together, and even more how we became parents together.

But Oceane, it was the late seventies, the time of sexual liberation, women's liberation, and general revolt against the old establishment. I had left my teaching job in France and moved to Geneva to be with my boyfriend of the time, then had left him and was wondering what next. Exploring various possibilities had taken me to London, where I did a massage workshop led by a wild-looking, fun-loving man.

He seduced me and I was flattered, desperate for intimate connection. Oliver was lonely. We were two lost souls holding on to each other, and had the French language in common. I kept forgiving him.

Then your dad received an airfare from his mum to come and see her in Australia, where she had emigrated ten years before. This would be the beginning of a world tour for him, something he had been dreaming of. I thought that would be the end for us. But five days before Oliver was due to depart I realised I was pregnant.

He still left for Australia, and we agreed that we each had to make our own decision about keeping this baby or not. I decided I was ready to have a child, and my letter letting him know this crossed his somewhere over the oceans. He wanted to parent this child too.

So I flew to Australia to be with him and meet his family and we soon realised Australia was a good country to carve out a new life and raise our family. I loved that in Australia I was far away from my own difficult family. I had not liked England and he did not like France. So we stayed.

Before I knew it, we had three children under three and a half. It was beautiful to have the three of you, but it took its toll on our already rocky relationship.

We did have good years before it unravelled. We travelled well together and the adventure of exploring Australia kept us happy for a while. I never ever imagined in those early years that our relationship would become so toxic, Oceane, and so damaging to my beautiful children, caught up in the middle.

Friday 24 January 2003

Cécile

When I get home, you have arrived from the Bay a couple of hours earlier. I find you sitting at the computer and you hardly say hello. Reconnecting after your time away is not easy and takes a while. It is not that you push me away strongly. You let me look at the uni timetable you are organising for this year. You want to look ahead. Gradually you warm up, show me the photos of your holiday.

Tuesday 28 January 2003

Cécile

Today, the tears are close to the surface. The anguish is wearing me out. Oceane is struggling to find a reason to live. I sense from talking to the boys that they are not doing well either. It is more exhausting and overwhelming than ever before. I fear that they could act against their own lives instead of working through their difficulties. After all, suicide is contagious. There is a known copycat effect. It is as if once the taboo of suicide is broken in a family or group, any vulnerable parent, sibling, friend, even the guy down the road who hears or reads the news, is at risk.

The first thing my therapist, Isabella, asked me when I went back to see her for help was whether you knew about my sister Odile's suicide. Yes, you knew, it was occasionally part of our conversations, one of the family stories, an important part of my past. I still do not know whether such stories should be hidden from one's children.

Odile's suicide was precipitated by learning of the suicide of her own analyst at a time when she was extremely fragile. 'If he cannot live then how can I?' she wrote in her goodbye note.

Not long after her suicide, I let myself slip off the main rafter of an uncovered farmhouse roof. I sort of just let it happen. I did not come to any harm: my hands reflexively closed around the rafter as it was just above my head and I found myself hanging from it. Maybe I did not want to destroy myself after all.

'Your suicidality was unconscious, unlike Oceane's and Odile's,' explained Isabella.

Oceane, I need reassurance from you. If only you could tell me: 'Cécile, I am here and I intend to stay around.'

Sunday 2 February 2003

Oceane

Rough day. Hard to write because it feels like it sucks me down into a vortex. I think this is one of my most suicidal days since last October. It just creeps up on me. Thought I was battling it, thought I was managing to stay away from this part of my mind, but I blinked and I fell into it.

It is not that every moment is bad, like it was last year – I have mornings, or hours, or moments of the usual fun, light, happy me, but I seem to trip so easily into the pit where I feel there is no hope, no point, no use and just too much pain. I never realised how physical emotional pain can feel.

All I can do is listen to my funeral songs and imagine my eulogies. I practise rewriting my suicide notes – they'll be different the second time round. I think I know more about what Cécile and the others will need to hear to cope with it this time.

Monday 3 February 2003

Oceane

Beautiful note from you today, Mama, with a sweet Leunig cartoon – puts so much into perspective for me, and makes me feel incredibly sad for you too. Not in a pulling, stressful, negative way, but in a healthy, safe sort of way. I am sure you have said sorry and acknowledged some of this before, but for some reason this letter makes me hear it.

It makes me cry to think how much grief and sadness you must be feeling. I've been so wrapped up in my own mind that I haven't really stopped to think just how big this is for you too.

I don't want you to feel bad, Cécile. I do love you (even if I haven't found my voice to say it out loud to you) and know you will do whatever you can to protect me. I do see you like a protective lioness when it comes to us kids.

I know you want to hear that I am OK. I still don't know whether I am or not though. When I have a bad day, I don't want to cause you the pain and worry of knowing that I am dreaming of death. When I have a good day I am distracted with life, and don't think to tell you. Or maybe I am too scared to tell you when I have a good day, because I don't want to give you a false promise of survival that maybe I cannot keep.

I am accumulating moments that say 'yes, it'll be OK', but I cannot quite tell you this yet.

Letter from Cécile

Dearest Oceane,

I've framed for you this Leunig prayer. I hope you like it.

With it I am saying, please, Oceane, stay with us and become a fighter for the cause of love and joy.

I can't tell you how much I feel sorry for not having protected you. I hope you give me the chance to help you recover from the harm it has done you and that we both learn from it.

You know, I never thought there would be so much fighting with Oliver after we separated, never. I struggled so much with how to keep my integrity. When to fight and how, when to get away to protect myself, how to protect you children, when to speak up, when to stay quiet. It hurts so much to realise you are a casualty of the situation and the mistakes I made, but I am always thankful when you tell me how it was for you and I can think more and hopefully learn better ways.

I wish I had found a more elegant way to fight for my integrity, without causing so much pain to you and

Julian and Leon. Not that I did not try, I hope you know that …

But for you, Oceane, in your own battle please do not turn against yourself and your own life. Why would your own life be less valuable than anyone else's? Why should you be violent towards nobody except yourself? You are such a beautiful, gentle soul, respectful of life – I am always in awe of the way you protect even the smallest insect who happens to be in danger, the way you could care for your horse with such total devotion. That is the way you should have been treated and were not. I hope you get through your struggle to find the will to heal and can become a lover of your own life.

Your mama who loves you.

Monday 10 February 2003

Oceane

Ben, Dina, Alice and I have been in our shared house for a few days and I am in love with it. It was stressful finding this home, battling the real estate world and also convincing Cécile that I would be OK, but we got there.

I drove up with Cécile, a rented truck loaded up, and we chatted about the year ahead. I talked about the subjects I wanted to do at uni, and about my plans for the new house.

I love my big bedroom. I love having so much space to hang my clothes and I've had heaps of fun putting photos on the wall and hanging decorations everywhere. One of my favourites is the little note I've written and stuck above my computer. It says, 'It will all be OK in the end, if it's not OK, it's not the end!' Makes me hang on.

It's the end of the day now, and I am sitting up in bed, wrapped in my doona. This home feels so safe and nurturing compared to college. I think it is the combination of us all living together – I feel part of a group. We've had the best day, playing on the beach with a soccer ball, falling into the water when we got hot, and stopping for ice cream on the way home. We've joked, laughed ourselves silly, played and mucked around. We are all feeling the freedom of being out of college – cooking real food, eating when we want, having a whole house and yard to roam in, rather than our little box rooms.

I can sense Cécile's worry at the moment. Her constant texting and phone calls remind me that I am not necessarily OK, which really spoils a day for me when I am having a good one. I know Cécile can't be expected to time her contact so that it happens when I need it. The reality is that when she contacts me in a moment when I am feeling life is worthless and too difficult, I push her away. It is too painful to hear from her then. So yes, I recognise just how impossible it is: I don't want her interrupting my good days, and I avoid her on my bad ones.

I had my appointment with Dr Robert today, and tried to talk to her about this, but I must sound like a whiney brat. I have no trouble talking on the surface about events, conversations or general descriptions. The hardest thing with Dr Robert is that she wants me to delve into everything deeper than I wish to. I cannot stand long awkward silences in these sessions, so I feel caught between this awkwardness and having to try to answer her probing questions.

This is why I prefer my near-weekly meetings with the lawyers. They ask me direct, factual questions. There is no scary silence in the conversations; I can answer without analysing or worrying about how to shape my response. I can be emotionally distant when I need; they don't probe for how I am feeling about something, they just want me to give the facts. I think it is the first opportunity in my life to say painful things out loud without having to worry about the emotions immediately.

The old question comes up pretty regularly with Dr Robert – 'Are you feeling suicidal?'

Good question – I just don't know the answer. I tell Dr Robert 'no', every time. My biggest fear is being forced back into hospital, and so there is no way that I will give anything away that might risk that. More and more I reflect on how traumatised I feel by the way I was treated in hospital and how quickly I lost any remaining sense of self or hope while locked up in there. But do I actually feel OK? Mostly yes, I think it's fair to say. Days like today, I feel on top of the world. I'm best when I am distracted, connected, focused. But then there are moments that crash over me like a huge wave, swallowing me up and tumbling me until it scrapes me across the sand and dumps me with a thud on the beach. When that feeling comes, it fills up my entire body and it is as much a physical sensation as it is an emotional one.

I'd like to be able to talk about it more, but I am a bit restricted. My friends who know what happened seem to find it hard to talk about it openly – it is like Ben, Dina and Alice want to focus on the new happy me, not revisit the scariness of suicide. Jaz is always great to talk to, but she is busy doing her degree elsewhere and we don't see each other regularly. And I don't want anyone else to know. It feels like my suicide attempt is such a serious and untouchable topic.

Another factor is the college telling people about my attempt behind my back – it made me feel shamed, and the people they've told don't want to see me or make eye contact if I pass them around uni. Now I protect my privacy fiercely. I can't bear the shame if people give me that look of judgement. This secrecy is mostly fine for me – it is how I like it – but sometimes I just want to be able to tell people what is going on in my mind. New thoughts. Realisations I have. The memories that continue to haunt me. I sometimes even just want to crack a few jokes with someone about it, but I worry that my humour would be seen as madness.

Wednesday 12 February 2003

Oceane

Today is full of big, big emotions: largely positive, but incredibly intense. I am feeling the warmth and love and hurt and fear of so many old friends who've known me since I was a child. They've all chipped in to buy me a new bed, and I am sitting on it, loving it. It is an unbelievably significant gift as now I can associate my bed with positive, supportive memories rather than memories of the assault or of lying on it bleeding.

I read the cards and messages that accompanied it. One sticks with me in particular, from Theresa and Chris. Their words are so beautiful – I can't even take them all in and even though I keep re-reading them, I get the sense I have miles to go before I really understand them.

Funny how I couldn't feel the love and support of all these people a few months ago – I'd put up too big a fence. And people don't tend to show you their love and concern if they don't think you need it. Cécile told me briefly about seeing Theresa just after she'd found out I was in ICU, and knowing this makes me feel extra emotional about reading the card from her and Chris.

Would it have been different if I'd thought all these people cared so much back then? Who knows?

Would I now approach these people if I felt like I was drowning again? Cécile asked me that recently, on one of her pop-in visits. She often comes with a box of food from the garden and an inquisitive look in her eye.

It is a hard question to answer. On a day like today, when I feel the full whack of all this love and care, then yes, I would reach out. The problem is that sometimes it feels like everyone finds it easy to gather around in a crisis, but then they all go back to their busy lives and forget about you. Would I still feel confident, another day, reaching out if I was at the bottom of the pit? Probably not – even though I pretend I would when Cécile asks.

I also have to shut friends out when I feel suicidal because it is too painful to reflect on their pain and sadness if I acted on it. Strange cycle in a way: I protect myself by shutting out the people who are most likely to help me in a crisis.

I need blatantly obvious, overt signs from people to tell me that they care – I think my sense of self has been so warped that I can't pick up on the finer signals. Somehow having a physical object – my bed – and the words spelt out in these cards means that I finally feel that these friends are genuinely worried about me and do care what happens to me. I hope that I don't lose this feeling too quickly.

Letter from Theresa and Chris

Dear Oceane,

This is a verse I first read the year I turned 14 and for some reason it is the verse that has remained with me most strongly over the years. In these more recent years as a teacher, I write these words at the beginning of every term's program.

For me they describe well much of life's journey:

The woods The path, straight and winding, known and unknown

Are lovely The beauty and delight of things loved and familiar, treasured and comforting

Dark The times of doubt, fear, despair. Of unloveliness, unlovedness

And deep The depths of mystery and the unexplained realms of the mind and heart

But I have promises to keep The exhilaration and challenge of being one, just for one, always for me and sometimes for others

And miles to go The ups and downs, ins and outs, the days and months and years ... the moments and fleeting glimpses of my journey, my life

Before I sleep The sense of the never-ending story of my life – the possibility of different states of being and wakefulness.

May the enfolding of your bed each night remind you
that whatever else, you are much loved.

Good resting, sweet dreaming,

with love from,

Theresa & Chris

Sunday 16 February 2003

Cécile

Today I breathe a little easier after meeting up with you and your friend Jaz at the march against the war in Iraq. You look so beautifully contained and quietly alive with your homemade sign: 'Bombing for Peace is like Fucking for Virginity!'

I hear joyful pleasure in your voice when you say how the sign has attracted attention and compliments. My little world is safer while the bigger one is going to an unjust, unnecessary war.

Saturday 1 March 2003

Oceane

I've been avoiding writing: a strange mix of distracting, wonderful moments with friends and dark days that render me useless.

Something triggered me yesterday. I was with a group of some of my old friends from college and one of the new students – I didn't even know his name – collapsed and died while walking back from the pub. I just cannot process the ease with which he died and how unachievable but tempting it still is for me sometimes. Why can't I just fall over and die? I feel horrendous guilt that he died without wanting to, while metres from him, there I was craving, craving, craving death.

Sometimes it is like I am a plane crash survivor, living with survivor guilt. Why am I alive when other, more deserving people have died? The coldness and harshness of many of the doctors, nurses and psychiatrists in hospital certainly reinforces that feeling. Some hid it well, but others were not afraid to let me know that someone who tries to take their life does not deserve any help to stay alive.

It was too much. I ended up lighting matches and holding them against my hands – I needed to feel the pain. First time I've wanted to feel pain since October; the thought has been intolerable until now. I don't want to rely on harming myself to cope anymore though. The sting of the burns made me realise that I need to either just go and find a way to suicide, or not hurt myself anymore. I can't do the balancing act in between.

Sunday 2 March 2003

Cécile

I wake up from an anguished dream in which you are covered with burn marks and I am left with a sense of danger, that something is going wrong. I cannot call you: it only annoys you and who knows, maybe you are fine, partying or fast asleep. Yet once more my body won't find rest.

I am going to offer you my sewing machine. Recently you have taken to sewing more, bags and other things, and I can imagine it might help take you away from the troubled part of your mind.

I SMS you:

'Can I bring you my sewing machine today?'

'Yes that would be good.'

'I'll be there this afternoon.'

A little trick to hopefully buy some life. You are not blind though: you accept the machine but hardly open the door.

Later you tell me: 'You know, Cécile, you were right to worry about me.'

'Thanks for saying it, Oceane; sometimes I think I am mad.'

'No, you were right.'

'I wish I could help you more.'

'I have to do it myself.'

I understand; I had to do it myself too.

Monday 10 March 2003

Oceane

Uni classes have started and I feel focused and energised, glad to have a goal and a pursuit again. I love these first few weeks, when there is no stress of assessments yet. It feels good to be organised, on top of my readings, planning ahead. A fresh flame has been ignited inside me and it makes my days so much easier.

The best part of my week is going back to see the lawyers. Knowing where to go and what to expect makes me less nervous and more able to enjoy the sensation of them fighting for me. I notice that I take extra care deciding what to wear when I go there, wanting to look smart and beautiful and also still myself. I feel, without a doubt, that these lawyers, and this process, will help me find myself in the jungle of despair that I've gotten lost in.

Today I arrive ten minutes early, mostly because I want to have the time to enjoy the view from the waiting area. I feel reflective looking out across the City, watching all the miniature people walking, running, talking, driving. The thought of them each having their own life, their own pains and joys, makes me feel more peaceful with myself. I wonder how many people out there are feeling suicidal; how many are having their last day or last moments on this earth.

The lawyers arrive, interrupting my thoughts. They are all warmth and smiles – bright-eyed, full of fight.

They have prepared a list of questions, mostly based on the information I gave them in our first meetings. They need to know exact dates, exact words spoken and, apologetically, they also ask some difficult questions about what happened with Seth, why it happened more than once, why I didn't say something sooner.

One tells me gently, 'I think you might need to report what happened to the police. I know it's been a long time, but it will be one of the first things questioned by the court.'

My anxiety rises. Speaking to the lawyers feels safe; in fact, it feels good. But speaking to the police? That is terrifying. What will I say? What will happen?

Cécile, I know that if I told you all this, you would jump at the chance to support and help me through this process – but it's easier to keep the status quo.

What I want you to know, so that you can worry a little less, is that I am in safe hands. I don't feel uncomfortable with the lawyers like I do in therapy. They are strong women who are asking this of me because they are going into battle with me. I can ride on their confidence and their sense of what is right and just. When they open a can of worms or overturn a scary stone, they surround me as I stumble through the answers and explorations we need to do.

We are preparing for a formal conciliation through the Human Rights and Anti-Discrimination Board. It feels good to see the words 'HUMAN RIGHTS' on all the legal documents. I am rediscovering what my human rights are, Cécile. I cannot even begin to tell you how much this is helping me.

Saturday 15 March 2003

Oceane

It is hard not to compare every minute of today with every minute of the same day a year ago. To start with, there was finding my car had been broken into and glass everywhere. All day I remember: Seth helping me clear the glass and following me back to my room. The sudden violence of him pushing me to the bed. My shock. Inability to make a sound with a pillow forced over my head. The struggle. The fear. The weight of him. My desperate fighting. My frozen voice. My utter confusion and the bile taste of panic.

Alice comes in mid-afternoon, asking how I am. I manage to just say that I am having a reflective day: 'One year on ... you know?'

She seems to understand but gives me a time limit: 'Well, you can lie here a bit more, but then at five pm we are going to get ice cream.'

Very Alice: blunt, but caring. She is protective of me and such a good friend.

Her bossy voice snaps me out of my moodiness and I feel strangely OK. Despite my wallowing, I haven't entered that dark space I know so well. I just feel a bit floaty, removed from my body, and there is a faint hum of adrenalin that is stronger than usual.

My flatmates have been invaluable at keeping me going. The relief of being out of college is palpable and is only slightly tarnished by wondering why I didn't do it sooner.

People – including the lawyers – have asked me, 'Why did you stay at college if Seth was harassing you and you didn't feel safe?' I wish I had a smooth response but the reality is that I don't really know why I didn't move. Partly it was money: I had been given a partial scholarship for my fees and worried how I would cope elsewhere. Then as I spiralled down, I felt so weak, vulnerable, disempowered, dirty, unworthy, that I couldn't see that it would be good for me to move, that I'd be safer, or that I even deserved that opportunity. Then there was also my reliance on my new friends for support – I'd only just moved to the City, and my new friendship group was being formed at college. I feared that if I did move, I would just be in another house, in the same emotional state, but without my friends around.

People also ask how Seth could have come into my room more than once. Why didn't I report it the first time? Why wasn't my room locked all the time? Why did I not ask who was at the door when someone knocked? I am just as confused by these things as the people asking. I have questioned myself about how this could have happened more than once. In fact, I obsessed about it so much that I ended up taking out the ensuing anger on myself. The cutting was not only about releasing the pain and hurt inside; one part was also about punishing myself and expressing my hate for myself for allowing it all to happen.

I wish people were a little more aware of how easy it is to read their facial expressions – when I see their confusion and lack of understanding about why I made a decision (or didn't) I hear a thousand judging words.

Saturday 12 April 2003

Oceane

After what feels like a month of highs, the world has come crashing down on me today. I feel overwhelmed by everything I am juggling. Work. Uni. TAFE. Work. Lawyers. Study. Class. Work. Yoga. Work. Therapy. It is ironic: by filling every minute of every day with a commitment, I am less likely to dwell or focus on negatives, but maintaining this busyness is draining.

I often think of Oliver at the moment – I've barely spoken to him since the weekend before my suicide attempt. It is just that I am fragile still, and I need to do whatever it takes to make sure that I don't tip back over the abyss. I don't feel it is safe to be around people who take my energy at the moment.

But as soon as I let myself start imagining how Oliver feels about it, how hurt or confused he might be by my silence, then it really undoes me.

Wednesday 29 October 2003

Oceane

One year of staying alive. I've been anticipating it for weeks – months, really. I got to a point, I think about two months ago, when I realised that I would make it. It wasn't a guarantee that I would never commit suicide, but I knew that even if it got really tough, I'd at least make it to this date. It was nice in a way, realising that. It made me stop worrying about how I was feeling. I could somehow relax knowing that I was going to stay alive until 29 October 2003. After that date, I'd re-evaluate. No promises.

I wish I had counted my good days and bad over the last year. I am wondering what the balance would be – which side would win? Life or death? Some days have been a rollercoaster though, with a dozen mood changes in as many hours.

The thing that has really changed in the last twelve months is my relationships. I have thawed from a long hibernation, in terms of friends. Despite the obvious ups and downs of being flatmates, I feel fiercely loyal and close to Ben, Dina and Alice. If it is possible to have three best friends, they fit the criteria. I think my best memories of the year are with them: late night swims, gourmet feasts, conversations over wine and a game of something.

In the last few months I've even made friends outside of our house. I met Hayli at the start of the semester in one of my psychology classes. I didn't think I had it in me, but I struck up a conversation and we hit it off. Hayli had just gotten married, and although barely older than me had a worldliness about her that I loved. She'd grown up in South Africa, called a spade a spade, and was overwhelmingly generous and caring. I buzzed all day after our first interaction. Then next class, I was overjoyed when she came and sat next to me. Some days, I have to remind myself that it is actually true – I really am a person with friends!

My relationship with Cécile continues to have its moments but it has changed so much over the year. I still feel smothered and I want to wave my arms around my body to indicate the personal space I need, but something has shifted. She has written me a beautiful little note marking today and instead of rolling my eyes, I feel loved and nurtured.

But despite all these positive growth events, I think it would have been easier (for me anyway) if my attempt had succeeded. The good things over the last twelve months haven't magically erased the bad. Thinking this way doesn't mean that I'll go and kill myself tomorrow. Since I am alive, I will have a good shot at it and live as full, big and happy a life as I can. But if I decide to stop living, I think that will be easy to do. Death didn't scare me a year ago and it still doesn't.

Thursday 30 October 2003

Cécile

Oceanette, I have just woken up with the words 'one year'! A celebration. You have survived that long.

Oh, I know you are not out of the woods yet. I wish you had reached the other side of darkness, but one year is one year.

I see both your passion and your life-and-death struggle in the way you live so ferociously, doing far too much – your uni study, sign language course at TAFE, friends, work, lawyers, the lot ... Another form of killing yourself? I hope you do not burn out.

I'll be leaving the Mountains soon to bring you your present. Are you expecting me to mark the day? I hope you like the poster. I hope you'll hang it so that you can see it from your bed when you wake up and when you go to sleep, and that Chagall will speak to you in your dark moments.

Friday 14 November 2003

Oceane

I've got an appointment with a plastic surgeon today.

I came up with the idea a few weeks back, partially due to all my 'twelve months on' reflections. I want to prove to myself that I am planning for the longer term in my actions as well as my thoughts.

The surgeon is a lovely old, gentle man. Very much like a grandfather. He is delighted that someone has recommended him, and looks really chuffed, which endears him to me instantly. He becomes more serious as I tell my story, reminding me of Dr Loxton, my old GP back home who I saw when I came out of hospital. He has the same gravity and slight sadness in his eyes and no judgement.

It is hard to be making these kinds of decisions in the middle of uni exams. I haven't seen Dr Robert for therapy in over a month, because I felt it distracted me and took too much time out of my day with all the study that I have to get done. But I feel like I've just replaced her sessions with things like this appointment.

It is a pretty scary operation. Basically it involves him cutting away the scar tissue and removing the whole area of scarring on my wrists and forearms, then cutting out a patch from the back of my thigh and grafting it onto my wrists as new skin. Because it is a skin graft, just like they do for burns, there is a risk that my body will reject it, and I'd be left with a far worse situation. The surgeon says that if that did happen, I'd likely lose the use of my hands completely because the scar tissue would grow back so thick and inflexible. There is a sad irony in hoping my body will not reject the graft as I have rejected and hurt it.

It also means a general anaesthetic, a few days in hospital and being in a wheelchair or crutches for six weeks while my thigh recovers from having such a large section of skin removed.

The end of the conversation is more fun – the surgeon joins me in trying to make up a story I can tell everyone to explain the new scars that I will have. The winner is 'I was taking a big tray out of the oven full of delicious roast pumpkin and I accidentally tipped the hot oil onto my wrists and burnt them'. That would explain why I have two matching skin grafts, one on each forearm.

Because of the recovery time (arm in plaster for eight weeks, leg in half plaster for six weeks) I plan to do it in the summer holidays. It will rule out swimming at the beach, but I am so self-conscious of my scars that I avoid swimming in broad daylight quite often anyway.

Monday 1 December 2003

Oceane

Of all the new things this year a boyfriend was not what I expected. Not that I haven't been thinking about it. It has probably been the most significant recurring thought in my mind after one, suicide and two, court. I have been too embarrassed even to write about it, especially because it gets jumbled with everything else that has been going on in my head about Seth and boundaries. I've been very hesitant about getting back into 'dating' or any of the other stuff that everyone else my age seems to be doing. I have always known that it wouldn't suit me to sleep around or have meaningless one-night stands, but that does not mean that I haven't wanted a boyfriend.

And now there is Sam. He came to our house about a week ago. Ultra charming, confident and boyish. He is Alice's friend and was immediately adopted into the household, sleeping on Alice's floor. The day he came, I was the only one home, panicking about my last exam of the year. I was wearing my favourite green skirt. I was instantly charmed and went straight to the usual question, 'Could he be my boyfriend?'

Anyway, Alice started bringing home her boyfriend and Sam needed a new floor to sleep on, which ended up being the other half of my big bed. The first few nights we were just friendly – although I was beyond thrilled at having this gorgeous boy sleeping in my bed. Then last night, after lights out, we ended up kissing.

I was so scared waking up this morning, that it would all have been a dream. Or even worse, just a momentary misjudgement on his part and that he would regret having started anything. But after he woke, he sleepily turned to kiss me – phew.

So today I have been on the ultimate of highs. I feel gorgeous, sexy and light with happiness. I want to tell everyone I know about Sam, and find it so hard to play cool. It is just delicious, this feeling.

And the best bit is that I didn't have the slightest hesitation or worry when we were kissing. The last two dates I went on fizzled out only hours in. One boy I felt so uncomfortable with that I dialled a friend from the toilets and begged her to call me in five minutes and fake an emergency. The other was just awkward, and when he tried to kiss me at the end of the night I felt no interest or emotion whatsoever. I was starting to think that maybe I'd never be attracted to anyone.

But it is different with Sam – I don't have any fears. I even told him about my suicide attempt and battles last night, before we kissed for the first time. If anything, he is more fearful than I am about it all. Worried that he will make me scared or uncomfortable. It is funny to be the one reassuring him that I am totally fine – seriously totally fine with kissing him. The only strangeness for me is that I have no desire for anything more than kissing.

Hayli came around later and danced with me in excitement – we giggled and gossiped together about this thrilling news. The euphoria is doubled because I have finished exams and can just enjoy the bliss of summer holidays and the long weeks ahead of wondrous boyfriend-filled days.

Thursday 8 January 2004

Cécile

Ma poulette, how are you feeling about tomorrow? It cannot have been an easy decision to undergo your first skin graft, with the huge risk involved. You know, Oceane, I wanted to try to pull you away from this one – I thought it was too risky, but you had the usual 'nothing will make me change my mind' determination and all I could do was go along. I have even resorted to praying to a god I don't even believe in: 'She is such a good person. God, you have to treat her well.'

You do not want me to take you to the hospital or pick you up. You have organised everything with your friends. Oceanette, I never know whether this independence of yours comes from your anger or from your healthy self who has her own mob looking after her.

Tuesday 13 February 2004

Oceane

It's been three weeks since my operation – I still shudder remembering the pain and the awful post-anaesthetic feeling. Today is the first time that I am out of the wheelchair; I am not supposed to put weight on my leg yet, but it is kind of OK if I use a crutch under my good arm, and just hobble with the lightest pressure on my bad leg. I don't make it far, but at least I am not reliant on someone pushing me in the wheelchair.

The big news today is that we have new flatmates. Ben and Dina moved out last week, and two new girls have moved in. One is Kat, an American exchange student who works at the same restaurant as Sam. The other is Katie, who was keen to move out of college after two long years there.

It is nice to have a change of guard in our shared house – I've loved the foursome we had going, but I also love the potential for new friendships, with Kat especially. Her bouncy black hair matches her bouncy personality and although I'm sure she has a more serious and vulnerable side, she seems to have a constant smile on her face.

Hayli has been around heaps too, helping me out, especially when Sam is at work. She is truly amazing and she and Kat seem to have hit it off – I can feel my group of friends expanding and I love the feeling.

Saturday 21 February 2004

Oceane

I've been crying all day – I'm totally exhausted from it. Finally curled up in bed, trying to get rid of the day. Kat is in my bed too, keeping me company – she's become an instant best friend.

Kat came home from working at the restaurant totally distraught. She'd been in the bathroom when another waitress came in and excitedly told her that she'd just had the most amazing night – with Sam. The same Sam who is supposed to be my boyfriend.

When Kat told me, I just burst into tears. I was disappointed by the actual deception and shame of having him cheat on me, but also because it meant I no longer could say 'my boyfriend'. We hadn't been having sex, which for most guys might have been an issue a few months into a relationship, but seemed fine for Sam. He was keen to be gentlemanly and wait till I was ready – he said so many times that he completely understood my need to take it slowly.

I am too exhausted to write every detail of the day. Hayli came over straight away and looked after me and I had a chat to Sam – he came home in the afternoon, and he started denying it but it was pretty obvious what had happened. So he is gone and I feel like a total failure as well as a blubbery, ugly mess.

Wednesday 31 March 2004

Oceane

I think I am feeling a bit strange today because of my dream last night. It has only been a few weeks since I've started remembering my dreams again, and each time they have been crazy and vivid and weird. This one has really shaken me. In it, Cécile, out of the blue, told me that she had a brain tumour. Then she started hallucinating – she'd be normal for a few minutes, then suddenly do something totally crazy. I was trying to take her to emergency at the hospital but she kept running away from me and stripping naked. I remember at one point, I was carrying her across a muddy field; she was naked and incredibly thin and frail.

It was so distressing, but I also felt like I woke up lighter in my body. Like I had cried and released sadness that I couldn't access when awake.

I can see this dream relates to my sense of being the one 'carrying' Cécile at times in my childhood, but it also gives me a taste of how it feels to be so worried and sad about someone you love. In the last months it has been Cécile carrying me through the muddy fields.

Despite the lightness I feel, the emotions in the dream have drained me. It's been an intense week with the lawyers too. I've been there nearly every day, and suddenly I've got to make enormous decisions about the direction of the case. There is so much at stake financially and emotionally.

Saturday 3 April 2004

Cécile

Oceanette, a quiet moment in the afternoon. You have offered to drive Leon back to his place.

It's been nice to have the two of you at home for the weekend. I love the early 'Mama!' call you both still give me as you hear me potter around the kitchen, and the big hugs still full of your warm sleepiness to herald the new day. It brings back the similar moments of your early years.

Do you remember the photo of you and Leon lying together in an old wheelbarrow? You were almost three and Leon just four; we were living in our caravan by the river. There was so much pleasure in your faces as you cuddled together, your naked bodies all plump and golden from years of living outdoors.

I wonder how you and Leon are going in the car. It sounded like you were going to have a long overdue brother–sister talk about the year that tore up your relationship.

Oceane

I woke up in the Mountains this morning, after getting a lift back from the City with Cécile last night. Good to wake to the homely sound of Mama doing her usual morning pottering around. I love the familiarity of the sound of the water system kicking in and the creaks and groans of the house. Even the feel of the bed and doona and sheets has an intense familiarity. I remember enjoying these sounds and feelings in the first few days after coming out of hospital just as much as I did this morning.

I am on my way back to Cécile's now after driving Leon home so that we could have a chat. He's been badgering me for a talk. He listened and didn't argue as much as I expected. I think Leon and I left the conversation feeling we'd both had our say, but not really agreeing or understanding each other either. Not sure if it was good or not.

We were talking about our year in the Capital, when we shared the flat. We realised a few months ago that this was the real breaking point in our relationship and he wanted to analyse it.

It was difficult to describe what that year was like for me – day after day of him and his friends, the drugs, the smell, the noise late at night, the messy house, the frustration of trying to talk to someone who's always stoned, the worry about money and bills. We were both so young to be living out of home, but I think I had an expectation that he would look out for me somehow, or at least look after himself. Whereas the reality was the opposite – I felt like I had to look after both of us. I couldn't articulate or draw the link for him between some of the things that happened that year and the repetition of me once again feeling unsafe, like I had to be the carer, the quiet one, the good one.

I'd been so excited when Cécile and Oliver had supported my decision to move to the Capital. I had sold the idea under the guise of the improved education I would get, but the reality was that I needed a fresh start. I felt increasingly trapped at Oliver and Miranda's house, but I felt I couldn't return to Cécile's – I did not think our fraught relationship would cope.

But it was my relationship with Leon that broke down in the end. I remember after one particularly bad night saying to myself that I would never trust him again. It made a permanent scar on our relationship.

I remember how much strength and pride I felt at moving to the Capital so young. I loved the shocked reactions I'd get from teachers when I said I had to sign my own absence notes or permission slips as I lived independently of my parents. I loved how I could nonchalantly shrug and say 'it's no big deal' when people commented on how I could pay bills, cook, clean and do my last two years of school on my own. Leon's behaviour was like a wrecking ball that year and I can't let go of how he robbed me of the self-esteem and gratification I had started to feel in my independent life.

The hard thing is that from his perspective, he wasn't really responsible for his actions. He genuinely feels that it was external factors (like our family history) that caused his behaviour, ergo, not his responsibility. I know I am being somewhat unforgiving and hanging on to the memory for too long, but I don't know if Leon really understood how affected I was, and how much I needed space after that.

Wednesday 14 April 2004

Oceane

Another meeting with my lawyers today. Mostly we re-covered old ground, preparing for the conciliation meeting with the anti-discrimination board and talking about the potential outcomes. The college reacted badly to our letter outlining what we were hoping to achieve from the meeting. It felt like their lawyers were trying to force me into running a civil case instead of an anti-discrimination case by saying that what I wanted from the conciliation was so outrageous that they didn't think it was even worth turning up.

I find these legal decisions tough. Running a civil case is expensive – and I don't want to appear like a gold-digger. The discrimination angle allows me to seek resolution for their actions towards me. Sometimes it just seems too complicated.

In their response to my lawyers, the college also made a mild threat, saying they 'know lots of things' about me, meaning family stuff. So the lawyers have been trying to prepare me for how nasty things might get.

I am so upset by them bringing up my past. I was doing OK before the assault. Despite the ups and downs, I was actually managing my family stuff. It never made me feel suicidal. Frustrated? Yes. Angry? Yes. Vulnerable? Very much yes.

I'd had rough patches in my life before, but what happened at college – how they responded to the assault so flippantly, nearly mocking me – drove me to self-hate, and that was what became so dangerous in the end.

But there is a little voice in me that screams with frustration at my family: 'Haven't you made it tough enough?' I already had to survive it once. Why does this history have to keep haunting me?

Friday 25 April 2004

Oceane

Best day. Best, best day.

So much has changed when I look at where I was on my eighteenth birthday compared to my twentieth.

I have friends!

They bounced on my bed this morning – Alice, Kat, Hayli. Bringing presents and breakfast in bed. Even a little flower on my breakfast tray. The sun coming in the window looked brighter, the air looked clearer and smelt cleaner.

I have activities I enjoy!

We went out to the beach – climbing the rocks and looking over the beautiful ocean at the waves crashing in. It was just lovely to hang out and enjoy everyone's company. I even got taken to the stables for a birthday ride. I've missed horseriding so much over the last few years.

I feel the love and support of my family!

I had a really nice catch-up with Cécile, Julian and Leon – it is strange and new after so many years of feuding to be able to do things with Julian and Leon together. I felt so celebrated for my birthday. Amazing when I look at Cécile and me now. The animosity is gone – there have still been difficult conversations and it is still hard to balance what she wants from me and what I can give in terms of personal disclosure, but it is much better.

I have plans for tomorrow!

That is a big change compared to two years ago – even one year ago, really. I have PLANS. I can picture tomorrow. I am catching up with the girls from TAFE. They are my slightly quirky friends – all a bit left of centre and we have a lot of fun together. Sometimes we practise our sign language, going out and ordering and speaking in Auslan. I sense they somehow know that behind my cheery smile there is more pain and vulnerability than I let on.

Happy Birthday, Me. Another year survived.

Thursday 29 April 2004

Oceane

It's taken me until today, but I finally told Hayli and Kat about the legal stuff. That the conciliation meeting didn't work out how we hoped, and now it might only be the beginning of a federal court case.

They were great – of course. I didn't expect them to be anything else. It was just their disappointment for me that was hard to see. It hurts to see your own emotions reflected on someone else's face. I felt so shattered when the conciliation fell apart that I haven't even had it in me to write what happened. But talking to Kat and Hayli gave me the confidence and energy to go and pull together all the information and documents needed for the Federal Court application. I managed to lift my mood by dropping all of it off to my lawyers and coming to a cafe to study for the afternoon – it's nice to be out of the house. In the cafe's courtyard, I see miniature flowers trying to grow in the cracks between the old bricks and I silently describe them to Oma, who reminds me often to make sure I see something beautiful every day.

Sunday 2 May 2004

Cécile

It is night. All is quiet inside the house and outside. I am sitting at the low table in my bedroom – my writing corner – when the phone rings.

You let me know that you are at the door of a big, big decision that weighs on you. You need to decide whether to go all the way to the Federal Court.

My God! How can such a young person have to make such a big decision? I see images of you tackling not only the dean and master of your college, but the whole church that backs them up, and also those wigged, black-gowned judges who can look so dusty and non-human.

'I am not sure what to do.'

'What are the risks?'

'If I lose, I'll have to pay all their court costs, a huge amount.'

You do not have that money, Oceane. I do not have that money. But I understand this is not about money really; it is about justice, about recognition of the way the college has mistreated you. It is about wanting to help other young women who have been, and will be, sexually abused at college. You want the college to be forced to change their procedures. It is about not letting these guys get away with it, simply because they are older men and have the money behind them. They have tried to crush you, have not thought twice about resorting to bad faith – not bad for 'people of the faith' – to prove that your suicide attempt had nothing to do with them. To them you are an annoying insect and they want to swat you away or crush you.

Oceane, can you become the gnat in the fable by La Fontaine, who is actually more powerful than the lion, king of the forest?

I wish I could tell you what to do. What I want though is for you not to end up crushed.

'You know, it is sad and wrong, but court cases are not always about fairness.'

You become quiet, poised to listen to more.

'You know, sometimes court cases have nothing to do with justice. Sometimes, it is the people with all the money to throw into the case who end up winning.'

'I know,' you say with resignation in your voice. 'But I think I have to try. I have come so far now.'

A new silence. You seem to hesitate. 'If it goes to the High Court, it will become public. They have to publish all the proceedings. Anyone could read about it on the internet.'

Oh Oceane, what a dilemma. I remember how it all went so wrong after you had the courage to report the assault. These two guys, the whole Church in fact, are ready to drag you back down into your death. And yet, and yet, I can see how winning the case would airlift you a long way into life.

'Whatever you choose I'll be there and do all I can to help you.'

Oceanette, I pray to the universe that you do not get crushed again.

Monday 3 May 2004

Oceane

My life revolves around the lawyer routine. Once, twice, thrice a week I make my way to their office. I greet the receptionist, who chats comfortably with me now. I have my five-minute meditation: utter peace as I look down at the world from the forty-second floor. The fact that the world below is miniaturised helps me see the big picture – not just focus on my little world, my hurts, tough days and sometimes blinkered existence. It is uplifting. All these people. All these lives below rushing around.

One uncomfortable conversation today, with Miranda. She was upset because it is nearly the two-year anniversary since she and my dad separated.

Our lives are strangely intertwined and yet we have very different events to reflect on from the last two years. She plays a much bigger part in my life than I ever imagined she would. She gets me in a way that others in the family rarely do, and often sees through my shield and understands what is happening in me. Also I'll be forever grateful for the fact she shared her family with me when she came into my life.

Sometimes I wish that I was better at expressing my needs. If only I could have told Miranda: 'Look, I am sorry that you are sad about the fact that you and Oliver divorced two years ago, I am sorry you are stressed about money, but this isn't a great time for me to talk about your problems, and as you are my stepmother, supposedly senior to me, I don't think you should tell me about all your problems.'

She doesn't know about the court case, so I can't really tell her that I am stressed because of that. It's hard keeping it a secret from so many people, but I still can't just talk about it like a normal person would. Privacy feels so much safer, and it is also simply a habit, I think.

Sometimes I feel like a garbage receptacle for everyone else's problems in the family.

Thursday 20 May 2004

Oceane

Such a great day! I have arrived in the Bay – just when I felt like it was all becoming too much and I was about to hit the wall and fall down into a big black hole. But I got here in time to be rescued. Straight into big loving hugs. Sometimes I wonder if I let myself start to fall when I know I am on my way to the Bay. I've been coming up every three or so months and I feel like this every time.

Today was extra amazing because I visited my beautiful horse, Freya, who is on 100 acres of hilly bushland, rainforest and paddocks. She arrived a year ago, but between weather, my skin grafts and time constraints, it has taken till now for me to do the extra two-hour drive to go and see her. Mieke, her friend, who owns the place, and I went for a bareback ride – speed, madness and joy mixed together. I was on Freya of course. We galloped and galloped. We jumped over logs, ducked under tree branches, splashed through creeks. The horses were all wild. Beautiful. Free. The sweat and dirt became as slippery as black ice, and it was sheer adrenalin that kept my thighs clamped tightly enough to stay on Freya.

After one long, long gallop up a hill we all stopped at the top to let the horses puff out their heaving chests. We happened to be under a sweet lemonade tree and Mieke plucked a lemon and tossed it to me. By some miracle I caught it, and sat there, tearing skin off and sucking the juice. I don't have words to describe just how enlivening the moment was.

The Bay is so restorative. I love the drives chatting with Mieke, playing and swimming with the girls, dissecting and analysing things with Mieke and Hans over a late dinner, the girls already in bed. I feel autonomous, valued, engaged in life. I belong.

Friday 28 May 2004

Oceane

I had my appointment with Dr Robert today. I've been seeing her for a while now, and sometimes I worry that we are going round in circles.

She asked me to talk about how I reflect on my family. I hope I didn't make it sound overly good in a fake way. I got the sense she thought I was a bit in denial as I kept justifying the hard stories with excuses of 'but it wasn't all bad ...' 'but it wasn't their fault...' 'but I don't think he realised ...'

I talked about how Cécile's and Oliver's family histories shaped who they had become and the parenting style they adopted. For example, Cécile's ultra-conservative family made her want to give her children choice and independence. Then there is Oliver's mother, my grandma. Her memoir paints a picture of a turbulent childhood marked by poverty and multiple moves, her survival in the Holocaust, and her later trials and tribulations. I actually typed up the memoir for her years ago, so I know of every rape and trauma she experienced. Dr Robert asked me about the book launch at the Jewish Museum just before my suicide attempt and I tried to say how intensely guilty I felt about my own tramua when she had suffered such extreme abuse.

Talking of her leads to questions about my dad. It is hard to explain him to Dr Robert. There is so much in my head that I cannot say out loud. After Oliver and Cécile separated, I didn't know what to believe with all the horrible stories they would fling at each other via me. For years I took his side and felt it was my job to keep him happy. It seemed safer to be angry and distant with Cécile. I convinced myself that I loved the fun at Oliver and Miranda's house – and at least I was away from the boys there. But then the little cracks started to appear. And that is when I learnt to withdraw, to protect myself.

After saying all this to Dr Robert, I suddenly became really anxious. I am nervous of what might end up being subpoenaed by the court. I don't want all this stuff to be made public or dissected by the other side. I don't want to sugarcoat our family history or other life events that have shaped me in some way; neither do I want them to cost me this court case.

She also asked me if I'd forgiven Cécile. Tricky question. I think to forgive someone, you can no longer hold it against them. I don't know if I do that. Dr Robert said to forgive is to no longer regret the past. I don't know about that either.

I feel like I have come such a long way with Cécile. I don't hold the same anger and frustration, but have I completely let go? I generally do not regret the past – mostly I really appreciate a lot of our childhood, although I know it doesn't often sound that way. I love the freedom we had as kids, playing outside, all the adventures that we could have. I feel so lucky that I got to travel to France and connect with my cousins there. I am grateful we didn't have a television or video games to get stuck in front of, and that we grew up appreciating healthy home-grown food. Cécile and Oliver were good at listening to me when I said something important – like when I wanted to change primary schools or skip a year. Most parents would have probably ignored me, but Cécile and Oliver really made it happen when it was important. I did love all the camping and other holidays we went on even though they were sometimes fraught.

The parts I regret are more to do with my actions than anyone else's. I regret that I didn't speak up and do more to protect myself.

Looking back, trying to be objective and not focus on the frustrations, Cécile has proven herself to me again and again in the past year and a half. That goes a long way towards forgiveness. I sort of appreciate that she always did the best she could at the time, and she is showing me now that she can be the mother I wished for back then.

Although seeing Dr Robert has made me stop and think about patterns in my childhood and my relationship with Oliver and Cécile, I think maybe I will stop coming to see her. The court case stuff is too overwhelming, and I don't think I can talk freely with the threat of a subpoena hanging over me.

Friday 29 October 2004

Oceane

Two years today. Feels like a repeat of last year, anticipating and reflecting on the one-year mark. But a lot is different, I guess.

I've had and lost a boyfriend – as devastated and upset as I was about that, the funny thing is that I bounced back pretty quick. The sadness of my emotions didn't send me into any sort of downward spiral – suicide didn't even cross my mind when it all blew up. It was a healthy sadness, and it passed quickly, which makes me question how much I was in love with Sam or whether it was just the concept of having a boyfriend.

The house has changed a lot – Ben and Dina are living down the road so I still get to see them plenty, which is great, and their replacements have also become firm friends. Especially Kat – with her and Hayli from uni, I have had some of the best fun this year. Hayli brings life and joy into everything she does. She and Kat are such generous, nourishing friends. We've jumped in the car on the spur of the moment and gone on a road trip to the Bay to visit Mieke, Hans and the girls; we've organised wild weekends of fun for birthdays and other celebrations.

My dark moments still sneak in sometimes. If there is a little crack that appears in one aspect of life – a moment of tension between the flatmates, a delayed response to a text message from a friend, even not receiving an email when I am waiting for one – I can spin out with loneliness, self-doubt and then harshness and anger towards myself. But I recover quicker from these moments. I don't physically hurt myself anymore, even if I still crave it sometimes. And the dark doesn't hang around; nor is it as dark or as deep as it once was.

I guess I'm less fragile now; it takes something bigger to overwhelm me. Even going to lectures and writing assignments on touchy subjects – PTSD, borderline personality disorder, child abuse or the impact of sexual assault – is easier to cope with than it was in 2003. I had to walk out of a few classes back then, when something hit too close to home, but now it just makes me a bit reflective and maybe a bit more moody or quiet for the afternoon.

If Cécile asked me today 'Are you glad you survived?' what would I answer? I'd hesitate. If I could press a magic button and somehow disappear from existence painlessly and without hurting anyone else, I'd still press it. I still have no fear of death. But I would find it harder to kill myself knowing what pain I would cause my family and friends. The other reality is that I don't think I could hide suicidality as easily. I am so much more connected to people than I was a few years ago. I realise that I wouldn't just rot slowly in my room not to be found for days or weeks. People would notice, and that feels pretty good.

Although I keep thinking of this court case as the fork in the road between life and death, maybe I've actually been on the right path for longer than I realise. Maybe I have enough strength and hope and tenacity to hang on no matter what happens.

Wednesday 10 November 2004

Oceane

Today is the big day. I am going to court. I left for the City bright and early – in a new skirt and top – and met up with my lawyers at their office. Like the first day I met them, they were all bright-eyed, laughing and ultra chic. I was slightly calmed by them, but still jittery, shaky and sick to my stomach.

I have to keep reminding myself: 'This is the moment. Remember how all year you thought it would never arrive and it was so far away? Well, this is it. Stop. Be present. Remember this moment. And this moment. And this one too. Do not skip ahead, just take the day one breath at a time. Soon it will be behind you.'

We are given a little room to set up in. I can leave my bag with the lawyers' paperwork there. We've chosen a trial by judge rather than jury, mostly for my sake, to maintain more privacy and dignity. The start is similar to last time, but it is a Federal Court judge in front of us this time. The courtroom is not what I expected – I had in my mind the typical TV show courtroom with the big bench and aisle and chairs and witness box. Instead, it is just a plain room with the judge at the front and the two parties sitting at a table more or less opposite each other.

The judge looks Italian, and has a stern expression that relaxes into a friendly one on a regular basis. It is like he knows that his default expression is a little intimidating, and he has to remind himself to look a little friendlier so as not to scare me.

The lawyers snap into their professional mode. They have all the right words – 'Your Honour', 'if it pleases'.

Before I've finished processing the surrounds and the new faces on the college's legal team the opening statements have started. There is nothing new in my lawyers' speech, but obviously the college's side is uncharted territory for all of us. There are no huge surprises – they go in strong on the attack about my family history.

My job is to be silent, till questioned. This is incredibly hard when someone is saying things in front of you that you want to prove wrong, or challenge. I don't know what to do with my face while they are speaking – I don't want to roll my eyes or grimace, but nor can I smile or nod like I can when my lawyers speak. And if I keep a neutral expression, I feel like I might be judged for being devoid of emotion. The pressure builds up in me and it is really hard not to explode with tears.

The next part is the witnesses' affidavits. My lawyers have interviewed my old high school friend Jaz and also Annemaree, as she has known me since I was five. They've both said that I was fine in my teen years. No evidence of suicidality. Annemaree also confirmed details of the meeting she was at with the dean and master of the college.

To counter this, the college has put forward testimonies from Bonnie and Angie – the two people I confided in during my first year of college. Silly me, thinking they were friends. This brings up memories of loneliness and shame, and my increasing reliance on these two throughout the year. As good Christians, they were so friendly and open with me. When the assaults happened and I told Angie, she bent over backwards to check up on me, chat with me, bring me chocolate or invite me out for coffee. I fell into her offer of friendship with the desperation of a starved child. And now it is all slapping me in the face. Every conversation or email exchange, every sobbing, messy piece of information I shared, has now been spouted out into this court.

I have to blink back tears because I feel so mortified and embarrassed. It is a combination of the fact that I made a bad call choosing these friends to confide in and simply hearing my secrets and innermost thoughts publicly shared. I feel bad too that this is making the work harder for my lawyers. I can't help but wonder, 'Do you think less of me now after hearing all this? Do you think that I am not the person you thought I was?'

The judge grants us a ten-minute recess after this – I think he noticed that I looked upset because he also said that he'd forgotten to mention at the start that if at any time I needed a bit of a break, to just let my lawyers know and they could ask for a recess.

I'm glad for the break; I feel so drained. The lawyers are good in the break and talk me through what the morning's events mean – in a language that I can understand better. They ask me a few questions about things that came out of the college's opening arguments so that they can respond, and then pretty quickly we get called back in.

Next on the schedule is me. I get the chance to say something to the judge and the two from college. I feel like I stuff it up though – fumbling, being repetitive and getting myself off track. I think I am just too nervous.

In the afternoon it is time for me to answer questions – both from my lawyers and theirs. I am somewhat prepared for the type of questions they will ask, but not at all for the level of aggression and hostility from the other side. Apparently, my lawyers tell me after, the college's new lawyers are known to be much more aggressive. It is not just the directness of their questions that is upsetting but their tone of voice – condescending, sarcastic, mocking. They try to blame my family, bringing up every event that ever happened.

The only saving thing in the questioning is the judge occasionally interjecting to tell the college lawyers that a line of questioning is inappropriate or that they should watch their tone. It boosts my morale enough to keep me afloat through it all. By the time the judge calls another recess, I feel like I have been dragged through hell for the better part of a few hours. I was actually physically sore in my body.

We are sitting in our own little room when the judge comes in and tells us that the college has made a settlement offer.

I am shocked. I had thought that by ripping me to shreds they were indicating that they were willing to fight this all the way. We still have to go back to the courtroom, and the judge still does a final address, even though he doesn't have to because of the settlement.

This is the glorious final hurrah for me. The judge speaks so positively and eloquently about the journey I've been on. He uses words that I didn't realise how badly I needed to hear, speaking about courage, and duty of care, and the strength it takes to make things right in the world, even if they are on a small local scale. He thanks me for the fight I put up to go through with this. I don't think he'll ever realise how much he gives me in this moment. It matters to me more than any settlement.

The judge's words give me back my dignity.

Sunday 1 May 2005

Cécile

Oceanette, we are celebrating your twenty-first today. You'll be driving up from the City soon with a couple of carloads of your uni friends. I have also invited my 'Mountain Circle' to join the party. We both have needed 'our people' so much over these last years.

When it is cake and presents time, I ask you to close your eyes and I place a tiny parcel in your cupped hands. Your eyes crinkle with anticipation. Not that you do not know what your present is. We have chosen it together. I wanted to give you a piece of jewellery to mark the occasion, both your turning twenty-one and surviving.

You decided on a ring you would wear all the time. And we found this stone called chrysoprase, an aeons-old stone from Western Australia, which a jeweller set for you. It is a green stone, with natural patterns and shades. It reminds me of the name I chose for you: Oceane – the power of the ocean combined with the femininity of water.

When I picked the ring up, the jeweller gave me this slip of paper that explained chrysoprase: 'A soothing stone. Fosters kindness and gentleness to yourself, brings a sense of security and trust, strengthens the life force and encourages hope.'

You read it now, nodding your head with each word, a wide grin on your face. We could not have chosen a better stone, could we? Then you read the words I had engraved on the inside – 'Love and life, Oceane, 25 April 2005' – and we hug.

Friday 20 January 2006

Cécile

All the lights are still on. The buzz inside jars with the summer stillness of the night. The house, instead of the usual neatness I like to leave it in before I go to bed, is in a mess. The kitchen table is littered with snaplock bags, plastic bags, measuring cups, half-empty gas cylinders we won't take.

We are packing our backpacks before heading off at dawn to start a week-long hike.

Julian's bedroom, which usually oozes that emptiness of rooms that are not used, has become 'the spot' for tonight. Everything we need – clothes, freshly dubbined hiking boots, billy, plastic bowls and mugs, hydration packs and much more – is laid out on Julian's bed and on the floor. Looking at this mess, it seems a miracle will be needed to fit it all in our two backpacks, which stand propped up against a chair in the middle of the room, top flaps thrown back, mouths gaping.

'I'll take the tent.'

'All right and I can take the trangia.'

On and on we go, stuffing our packs, making sure no air pocket is left. We weigh, we compare. Give me this, give me that. You end up with a huge backpack, Oceane, much heavier than mine. Are you realistic in regards to your strength or playing superwoman, enjoying the challenge and your youthful physical resilience, or looking after me in your matter-of-fact yet generous way?

We cannot afford to forget anything, or take anything superfluous as we'll be carrying all we need for seven days out there, tent and food included. Just the two of us, walking the far south-east corner of Australia, step by step. Neither of us has been there before, and it is not a signed track.

We've done hikes before. It is something we both love and do well together: the adventure, the challenge, the beauty of the Australian wilderness, the camps and nights in the middle of nowhere. You have just completed your honours degree with an unusual and original research project on deafness and brain damage.

Oceane, this will be such a different experience of surviving together to those first few weeks after your release from the psych unit. We have both survived, more than survived. We are ready to walk side by side just the two of us for a whole week. What a journey we've walked already, Oceanette. I cherish the new relationship we have built.

Monday 23 January 2006

Oceane

I haven't needed to write so much over the last year – I feel like I've been living life, rather than trying to analyse it or cope with it through writing. Cécile and I are on day three of our seven-day hike. After three days of utter wilderness, with seals on the beach, massive dunes, and estuaries crossed chest deep with bags on our heads, we've come to a little camping site which is something like paradise.

There is a bendy tree, growing horizontal, that we've hung our sleeping bags and tent over to dry out after the rain last night. Because we've had a shorter hiking day, we've managed to sit and put our feet up for an hour before needing to cook dinner and set up tents.

I am surprised to realise how very well we work together. Cécile has an amazing ability to pack my bag so that everything fits snugly and is well balanced. I can offer her some of my youth by carrying an extra five or ten kilos. She is the one to collect kindling and start the evening fire to cook on. I am the one to pitch our tent, lay out our sleeping mats side by side and neatly arrange our sleeping bags ready to be crawled into. She washes up. I go collect water. And the next day we do it all over again.

I love how strong and free I feel in my body when I am hiking. It has healed the fear and weakness and sense of being cornered that I felt in the hospital system all those years ago. Unpacking old boxes recently, I came across my hospital records that I had requested for the lawyers. That I didn't crumble reading them was a sign of how strong I am now.

This hike feels like it is marking the transformation of the relationship between Cécile and me. We are walking it together with a pretty arduous road behind us. It has been a gradual process over the last few years, but I feel like our closeness is suddenly out in the open and obvious to everyone. I am not trying to hide it and I am not ashamed to like my mum. I can actually tell people how much I respect and get along with her rather than fiercely try to pretend that I am an independent warrior who has survived a harsh and turbulent childhood.

There is something about the rhythm of hiking – the huge, heavy backpacks slow us down, forcing us to concentrate exquisitely on each step we take. There is such intensity in making sure that we don't tread on a snake, twist an ankle, trip on a branch, in keeping our balance as we leap from rock to rock or wade through the strong tide of an estuary pulling us to the sea. Somehow, that intensity and reliance on listening to my instinct makes everything so much clearer. It feels like I have opened up a little portal between my internal voice and my external voice and I am now able to articulate what is going on in my head. I don't have the hesitancy, doubt, secrecy, uncertainty that I have so often had with Cécile. The words just come out.

Among discussions of my future career plans, we also talk of my travel plans – I've booked my round-the-world ticket, leaving at the start of May. I am nervous, leaving my comfort zone and my friendships, which feel so solid at the moment. But I am ready to spend time with just my own company.

After so many years of running away from myself, or only speaking hatefully to myself, I am actually excited to just spend a year with me.

Tuesday 24 January 2006

Cécile

Today is an easy day, a breather halfway through our hike. We've been through magic nights and sunrises surrounded by dunes, through getting lost and not finding water, through hours along interminable beaches, struggling with the softness of the sand and southern winds from Antarctica, through charred forests under torrid afternoon sun. We've shared long talks and the silent intimacy of savouring each mouthful of our buckwheat, dried carrot and pea stew by the campfire, with tiny marsupials coming to share our meal. We've shared the intimacy of a tiny tent with only room for our two bodies, and the shock when a funnel-web jumped out of your sandal as you were slipping your foot into it to go for an early morning pee. Today we are doing the lighthouse to lighthouse part of the walk, a well-marked track, without climbs or rock scrambling. We have left our big packs at the camp, where we will return tonight, and the ease of the day is opening the space for deeper talking.

Your openness of last night is still with me. Oh, Oceane, if you knew how I love it when you trust me

313

with discussing your dilemmas, the questions that are bothering you, and also your dreams and plans.

I feel I have recovered my daughter, or maybe I should say 'found' my daughter. It means so much to me when you let me into your world, Oceane. I love listening to you, thinking aloud with you, asking you questions and hearing your answers.

Later this evening, as we eat our bowl of piping-hot polenta and dried tomatoes on the beach beneath our base camp, I am filled with the salty sea breeze, the sun and your trust. Thank you for a beautiful day, Oceanette. Sweet dreams.

Epilogue

Oceane

When, in 2010, I announced my plans for this manuscript to my mum and told her I wanted her voice in it, she took it in her stride. Literally. We were on a bush walk – our best connection time – puffing up a mountain.

For years I'd been rehearsing this book as a conversation between us in my head, with my side of the story built on memories, diaries, emails. I wanted to see what it would be like if I could also hear Cécile's voice.

Cécile had, in fact, been having the same one-way conversation with me, except that she had actually been writing it since a few days after she found me in hospital. It was her attempt to not freeze under the trauma.

When I sat at the computer, my story poured out. It was not hard to bring back to life the lost, confused, overwhelmed voice of my eighteen-year-old self. A few months later, Cécile and I were ready to share our respective pieces. I intertwined our two stories, putting them in date order. 'Let's just see if it works,' we said.

The first time we read our shared story, we were both blown away by how synchronous it was. Neither of us expected the intensity of our grief when we read each other's entries, nearly a decade after these events. But the process of writing every detail and then bearing witness to each other's experience brought an intimacy that we had never imagined possible for us.

I have to admit that I was shocked at the rawness of my emotions on that reading. I had convinced myself that it was so long ago and had no impact on me anymore. My skin grafts had healed well and there was little visible to the world of what I had done. But writing it reminded me that I do carry the history of these scars.

Cécile told me there is no magical finish line when it comes to processing trauma. You can't just leave it behind. For her, in writing, reading and re-reading, discussing, remembering more, letting emotions rise and subside while doing all the edits and re-edits, the trauma became an integral part of herself, of her story.

Writing and sharing it with each other was one thing, but publishing these words was not an easy decision, especially at first. For me, there was so much shame still associated with being someone who had attempted suicide. But the more we wrote, the more important it became. Suddenly everyone around us had a story of suicide, but I noticed nobody spoke about it until I opened the door.

We reached out to Pat McGorry, who had just been made Australian of the Year for his work in youth mental health. He wrote a beautiful foreword, expressing how important sharing stories like ours was for others – both professionals and families. This shifted something in us. But despite carrying a sense that it was important to share and speak our story, we weren't ready yet.

And then life carried on. We got distracted: I travelled the world, got a job, married the woman I'd fallen in love with; we built our home and started having babies. Cécile worked and travelled and hiked and moved to be closer to us and our first son. One day I decided to pick up our old manuscript. Now living a kilometre apart instead of 300, my mum and I began to meet at a local cafe to work on it when we could.

When I started, this book was very much just about suicide. To me suicide was the focus of the story and in some ways an easier focus than the more complicated elements of our family and intergenerational trauma, ideas around boundaries and what happened at college. I've since realised how much self-criticism and shame I've carried about being so affected by the difficult memories of my childhood and attempted rape at college. It is a strange and heavy guilt, feeling that what happened to me was so much less serious than what many other women go through. This feeling has been retriggered strongly, first with #metoo and then more recently with the news in the media about sexual assaults and the culture of harassment and silence in politics. It has been hard to look back over all the incidents in my childhood and early adulthood and accept that I don't need to justify if something was 'bad enough' or not.

In the process of writing this book, I've had the chance to reflect on the mental health system here in Australia and on the benefits and costs of mental health diagnoses and labels, and the stigma around all this. To me, 'coming out' about my suicide attempt is far more frightening than when I came out as gay after meeting Sarah.

When I first had contact with the community mental health centre, just a week or two prior to my suicide attempt, they tried to label me. Once I was in hospital being assessed daily or more frequently by a psychiatrist, it was the same. When I read their reports, years later, they used terms like 'major depression' or 'borderline personality disorder' when they discussed their diagnoses of me. Some people can feel relief at a diagnosis, and of course a diagnosis can be critical for correct medication and help for many people. But to me it just brought shame and exacerbated my helplessness, perhaps because they had a very medication-based focus at the time, and I felt that medication was not what I needed.

One of the longest lasting traumas has been some of the memories from my hospitalisation. How unsafe I felt there, how none of the overstretched psychiatrists seemed to listen till Dr Martin took the time to truly hear me. I've found out since that he was rapped on the knuckles for letting me out of the hospital, and I wish the system allowed for more humanity like Dr Martin had the courage to show me.

At the time, Cécile could only be a mother, but over the years as we've talked about my time in hospital and afterwards, she has been able to reflect with her therapist hat on about how challenged the Australian mental health system is. At the time, she felt strongly that the high-security psychiatric unit was not the place for me, and that the local community mental health centre that first saw me was not doing me a service by prescribing medication without adequate follow-up and investigation. At one point in her writing, Cécile wondered if mine was another case of antidepressants being given to young people without enough supervision, driving some of them to suicide. She felt so alone and let down when the community mental health centre made her feel scared that I had been discharged from hospital too early but would not provide any assistance. A Productivity Commission report into the mental health system released in 2020 articulates many of the issues I faced, and I hope the government stands by its commitment to overhaul the system. Although I write of my often-negative experiences in 'the system', I understand better now how difficult it is to be a nurse or healthcare worker in such situations.

My passion for change is as much about distressed and exhausted workers as it is about the patient. I have come across so many who do an amazing and often thankless job of caring for people such as myself in a system that does not make it easy for them.

Cécile wants to emphasise for other parents in a similar situation how important it is to have support. 'How can you hold a person on the brink if you are not held yourself?' she says. And she is right. Despite the challenges we had in 'the system', there were amazing people, friends, resources and services around us. It was just harder than we thought to find them. Of course, I wish I had spoken up earlier, asked for help from the friends I have since realised were so desperate to be there for me. But I also want to acknowledge how hard that can be. In the years since my experience, much has changed in the resources available, especially for teens and young adults. But I don't think we should ever stop advocating for more funding and focus on these services, to make them as personal and accessible and compassionate as possible.

While medication has a critical place in treating mental health issues, to me it isn't enough alone. Good therapy, reducing stigma in the community and accessible resources are just as critical. I think we, as a society, need to be less fearful of talking about suicide; I don't think media silence is healthy when we are trying to encourage suicidal people not to be silent about how they are feeling. Years before we found our agent and publisher, I did send the manuscript to a publishing house, who wrote back that it was a great book but there wasn't enough of a market for a book about suicide. That is hard to believe when we think about the statistics on suicide, let alone the family members, friends and community affected by each suicide. Increased awareness of mental health, particularly through COVID as well as the current media focus on large institutions attempting to cover up sexual harassment and assault, has certainly helped improve and open up the conversation. It feels like there has never been a more important time for my mum and me to finally air our once silent conversation.

Writing was one step, but the actual publishing process brought unexpected emotional challenges. I had not realised there would need to be so much compromise. Sharing the manuscript with my family turned out to be like throwing a litre of petrol on a spark, and the small amount of cohesion we had crumbled once more. I went from a complete high to an intense anger, rage even, that the men in my family were once more trying to silence me. I have had to accept the removal of both joyful memories and incredibly painful memories; however, it doesn't make what is left any less important. And I have to accept that what is left unsaid still happened and is of equal importance even if not included here.

Cécile and I both recognise how intense our story is, perhaps hard to read and unrelenting at times. But it shows that no matter how hard it gets, how deep and all-consuming the black hole of despair can feel, there is a way out of it. Despite the occasional fantasy of doing so, I cannot turn the clock back to when I – or Cécile – was a child or young adult and do anything about the fear or trauma. But I can say that I won't play a role in being silent about it now. And I hope this story will help others to not feel alone and speak up if they wish to.

Acknowledgements

Oceane

I firstly owe an overwhelmingly huge thank you to Dr Martin for listening to me that morning so many years ago. I am sorry I could never find you one year on to tell you that you made the right decision. Hopefully you find this note here instead. Although I talk of many negative moments in the health system, I can reflect now how impossibly hard it was for so many of its workers. I mean no disrespect or judgement on those that I criticised, and I especially appreciate the humanity shown in certain gestures, like the nurse who connected me to the internet or the paramedic who made me laugh. Likewise, I hope my magnificent team of warrior lawyers recognise themselves in these pages and realise just how vital their role was in my recovery.

Our gratitude for those who have helped bring this book to life is endless. So many friends cheered us on and read the manuscript. It is hard to mention some names without mentioning everyone, but a few mentions need to be made: Helen, Pippa and Joelle, our first big editors –

thank you for your meticulous and kind feedback. Liana, Sarah S., Hayli, Kaya, Anna, Blair, Brendan, Charlie, for your time reading and for your incredible friendship and support as we've needed it along the way.

Equally important have been those who helped us find enough courage to publish our story. In particular, the beautiful group of friends who have held us in the last year or so and provided so much support when we've needed it to keep going with this book. There are also many friends, both named, renamed and unnamed, who played a huge part in our life during the events we've written about – with the smallest and the grandest gestures. The compassion and help they gave us made an immeasurable difference. Sometimes it was as simple as a look or a hug you gave at the time. We hope you know who you are and how big your gift of love has been and continues to be.

In the last years, working on this book has also taken an enormous amount of time and energy – my wife, Sarah, gets our full gratitude for fielding the kids, providing the emotional support, and giving me the sense of security from which I found courage when I needed to. It is because of her love and the family life we have created that I feel I can bare these truths and tackle the shame and emotions in this memoir.

And last but certainly far from least: our manuscript was a bit lost before my friend Kaya got us in touch with our wonderful agent, Jane Novak, who possesses equal parts genius, patience and compassion. Likewise, we have experienced and benefited from truly magnificent care with the team at Hardie Grant Books, including Sonja for her wonderful editing, and above all Emily for her insightful contributions and for leading us with the most beautiful kindness through the exhilarating and terrifying journey of publishing. Thank you also to the patient and talented designer Laura Thomas and artist Angi Thomas for the beautiful cover – knowing this was a mother-daughter collaboration as well makes it extra special to hold our story within.

About the authors

Cécile Barral is the mother of three adult children, a grandmother, a gardener, a bush lover, a journal keeper and a psychotherapist with over twenty-five years of experience specialising in complex developmental trauma. Cécile is very actively involved in the Australia and New Zealand Association of Psychotherapy, has presented at multiple conferences and contributed to a number of books, and has a special interest in the use of writing to help process traumas. She emigrated from Europe to Australia in 1980 with a backpack, $100 and her first child in her belly, hoping that distance from a family plagued by mental health problems would protect her and her to-be-born children. She learnt the hard way about intergenerational trauma and believes working through her personal wounds has helped her become a good therapist.

Oceane Campbell is Cécile's third child and frequently wonders how Cécile survived living in a tent for a year with three children under three. Oceane herself has three children, and a beautiful wife, and is a proud and passionate midwife. She finds watching babies take their first breath incredibly life affirming after her struggles with mental health and a major suicide attempt in her teens. Oceane has published numerous midwifery articles and presented at many conferences, and enjoys writing in every spare minute on issues of consent, women's rights and autonomy. Before becoming a midwife, Oceane completed a psychology degree with honours and dabbled in less interesting jobs in mergers and acquisitions and policy writing.